4/28/04

CRM Unplugged

Releasing CRM's Strategic Value

Philip Bligh

Douglas Turk

WILEY

John Wiley & Sons, Inc.

Library of Congress Cataloging-in-Publication Data:

Bligh, Philip.
  CRM Unplugged : releasing CRM's strategic value / Philip Bligh, Douglas Turk.
    p. cm.
  Includes index.
  ISBN 0-471-48304-4 (cloth : alk. paper)
  1. Customer relations—Management. 2. Customer relations—Management—
Data processing. I. Turk, Douglas. II. Title.
  HF5415.5.B56 2004
  658.8'12—dc22

                                                                    2003025014

Printed in the United States of America
10 9 8 7 6 5 4 3 2 1

About the Authors

Philip Bligh is the Founder, Chairman, and CEO of Inforte Corp., a customer strategy and solutions consultancy based in Chicago. His extensive experience in customer, sales, and marketing strategy has established Inforte as one of the nation's leading and fastest growing strategic consultancies, with an enviable Wall Street reputation, including 20 consecutive quarters of profitability.

Under Phil's leadership, Inforte has a consistent track record of helping Fortune 1000 companies improve competitive advantage, market position, and profitability. Over the last decade, Phil's thinking around customer solutions has been applied at Avery-Dennison, Guardian Life, Home Depot, Sabre, Citibank, Wescorp, Toshiba, and many other top firms.

Phil, who is an author and respected speaker on the subject of customer strategy, has contributed to Harvard Business School Professor Michael Porter's articles in the *Harvard Business Review*. He has been interviewed by numerous media outlets, including *BusinessWeek, CBS Marketwatch, Chicago Tribune, The Economist, Financial Times, Forbes, Fortune,* and *Optimize Magazine* on topics relating to customer strategy and management.

Phil is an adjunct professor in management at DePaul University's Kellstadt Graduate School of Business and is also on the Board of

Directors for the Lyric Opera of Chicago. Phil graduated from University College of London. He lives in Chicago.

Douglas Turk, a recognized authority in customer, sales, and marketing strategy, has led numerous successful multimillion dollar customer strategy and solutions engagements for Global 1000 companies. Douglas is a speaker and facilitator at many of the leading industry shows and conferences and has been quoted in publications like *CIO Magazine*, *Computerworld*, *CRM Magazine*, and *Real Market* on topics relating to customer strategy and management.

Douglas is an Executive Vice President at Inforte Corp., a customer strategy and solutions consultancy based in Chicago. He manages Inforte's global sales and marketing functions and helps set the overall strategic direction of the firm. Douglas is a key member of an executive team that grew Inforte from $5 million to $64 million in four years. His contributions have helped Inforte remain profitable as a public company for 20 consecutive quarters and garner the honor of one of *Forbes Magazine's* Top 200 Small Businesses.

Douglas has served as an Adjunct Professor at Pepperdine University in Malibu, teaching entrepreneurship theory and practice. He holds J.D. and M.B.A. degrees from DePaul University and a B.S. in business administration from John Carroll University. He is also a member of the Board of Governors for The Hollygrove Home for Children in Los Angeles. Douglas lives in Santa Monica, California.

Contents

Foreword

In the euphoria over IT and the Internet in the 1990s and early 2000s, Customer Relationship Management (CRM) took center stage. Most every major company invested heavily in broad suites of demand side applications that were supposed to transform interactions with customers and drive sales and profitability. The logic behind CRM seemed compelling, and companies invested to the tune of tens of billions of dollars. Siebel Systems, among others, attained the status of a stock market darling as sales of software licenses grew exponentially. Huge CRM projects, reminiscent of enterprise resource planning (ERP) installations, became the dominant focus of many IT departments.

Unfortunately, the results fell far short of expectations. In fact, they have been downright disappointing. CRM failed to deliver the expected return on investment (ROI), if there was a ROI at all. What's worse, CRM installations at some prominent companies led to outright losses and damaged relationships with the very demand side partners that CRM was supposed to benefit. Because of these problems, many thousands of CRM software licenses have been put on the shelf or abandoned as companies lost faith in the concept.

What was the problem? It is tempting to label the whole idea of CRM a failure, but this would be a serious mistake. The aims of CRM remain highly relevant today, if not more so, given the relentless pressure of competition and the fatigue with diminishing returns of cost cutting. Clearly the problems with CRM were far more subtle, and far more multifaceted, than some observers would have us believe.

This book, drawn from the deep demand side experience of Inforte over the last 10 years, aims to both understand the historical difficulties with CRM and, more important, chart a path forward. With no ties to a particular vendor or technology, the authors bring a unique perspective that no software company can match. Having been involved in dozens of actual CRM implementations involving software from every major vendor, including remedial projects after initial CRM projects failed, Inforte has seen what works and doesn't work. Inforte is also in a unique position to go beyond theory and understand the organizational realities of technology planning and system of implementation, which prove to be major causes of CRM failures.

This book reveals how the past failures of CRM stem from multiple causes in both planning and implementation. There is no silver bullet that will guarantee success. Instead, a whole new way of conceiving of and implementing CRM is needed.

At the core of the Inforte approach is the notion that CRM is a tool for company strategy, not an end in itself. The book offers a textured understanding of how to align CRM with strategy, which has been almost entirely absent in practice. The book also goes well beyond technology planning to address the best ways in which companies should actually go about designing and implementing CRM applications. There is a wealth of knowledge here about the nitty gritty of successful software implementation that should be required reading for every manager overseeing this huge corporate investment area.

In the future, there is little doubt that every company will have to incorporate CRM concepts and technologies. The question is, who can do it in ways that not only deliver on the promise but actually result in competitive advantage. This book offers a comprehensive answer to this question that is eminently practical and actionable.

There are some who now argue that IT has become table stakes, and no longer a source of competitive advantage. The detailed history of CRM here belies this perspective. This book describes how a series of leading companies in a variety of fields have actually gained advantages from CRM—advantages that persist today. The book also reveals the complexity of this class of IT applications, which will make the diffusion of best practice in CRM slower than in many other application areas. At its core, however, the book demonstrates that competitive advantage from IT can result and be sustained where IT, whether it is CRM or otherwise, is applied in a way that is carefully focused and tailored to a company's unique way of competing versus rivals. This distinction, between viewing CRM as a generic best practice tool versus a strategy tool uniquely tailored to each company's approach to competing, is among the most important insights that must guide the future of IT.

Michael E. Porter
Harvard Business School

Preface

By any objective measure, Customer Relationship Management (CRM) has evolved into a useful collection of business approaches and technologies that help companies develop more profitable customer relationships. However, as happened with other good ideas such as the Internet, CRM got caught up in the irrational exuberance that led to the technology investment bubble. Companies spent too much on ill-defined technology efforts, and investors lined up to shovel money into technology stocks. The bubble inevitably burst and most were left picking up the pieces. As history clearly demonstrates, excesses often end in crashes, and crashes often over-correct for the past exuberance. Having swung too far one way during the run-up, the pendulum then swung too far back the other way and CRM fell into disrepute. It was widely branded as a failure and many organizations stopped investing in it.

Eventually, a more balanced perspective on CRM will prevail, but in the meantime, important opportunities are falling by the wayside. We wrote this book to help in restoring equilibrium, and to prevent the baby from being thrown out with the bathwater. *Implemented the right way, CRM delivers powerful benefits. It markedly improves the efficiency and effectiveness of sales, service, and marketing. But even more importantly, it can strengthen strategy and help generate enduring returns.* We hope to show how CRM should be defined, approached, and profitably applied to your business. We describe what went wrong and what lessons can be learned from the first phase of investment in CRM.

The title of the book—*CRM Unplugged*—captures a vital lesson that most early adopters had to learn the hard way: CRM really isn't about technology, it is about attracting and serving customers more effectively and more profitably. It is also about strengthening customer-related processes and activities in ways that fortify a firm's specific competitive advantages.

Instead of treating technology as the fundamental driver of this change, it should be considered an enabler of new policies, processes, and collaboration. It should play a supporting rather than a leading role in CRM. This is especially important since technology is typically expensive and investments should really be made selectively. Which raises another question: What exactly *are* the right areas to invest in? As we show in the book, the answer is actually quite simple: those areas that comprise the unique competitive advantages of your business. CRM's big punch is its ability to strengthen these advantages. Other areas might produce benefits too, but they will tend to be short-lived. Investment in the areas that create and enhance your competitive advantage result in sustainable gains for a simple reason: They are difficult for competitors to emulate.

Renowned Harvard professor Michael Porter has been the driving force in explaining how lasting competitive advantage is manifested in a business and sustained over time. In reality, his seminal works on competitive strategy and competitive advantage provide the framework for CRM, and indeed, all investment decisions. Inforte has worked on customer-related strategies and technologies for 10 years and we have spent much of that time doing what we can to influence decision makers to adopt the rigorous approaches recommended by Professor Porter.

Another aim of this book is to extol the need to treat all technology decisions as investment decisions, and to base them on firm strategy over anything else. In his Foreword to this book, Professor Porter relates his own experiences evangelizing this approach and offers vital advice for attaining and sustaining competitive advantage through CRM-related business improvements.

Inforte has had the good fortune to work with some of the world's leading companies on these challenges. Together with the highly talented people of Inforte, we have helped these companies to invest propitiously and implement wisely. Collectively, we have learned many lessons and we strove to pass along their essence in this book. *CRM Unplugged* was written for executives who shoulder the responsibility for making investments and delivering results. We understand you are busy and overloaded with information, and our aim was to condense our thoughts into a brief and readable format. We hope we have achieved this while adequately communicating our key messages. We also hope that your small investment in time with this book will be returned to you in spades via sustained increases in your profitability.

Acknowledgments

The book-writing process is a long and arduous journey that should not be undertaken without the support of many people. Through the course of the last year, we have worked with a variety of talented and dedicated individuals whose efforts have made this book possible.

We would first like to thank Steve Mack and Pamela Robertson. Steve's efforts and expertise on the topic did more than any other person to shape the book's ideas and structure. He provided essential thinking and content throughout the process. Pamela Robertson, Inforte's Vice President of Marketing, was both the guiding light and the backbone of the project. She provided exceptional guidance, review, editing, and encouragement. This book could not have been completed without her efforts. Director of Marketing, Craig Dooley, was also invaluable during this process providing the necessary research and support.

We also thank members of Inforte's executive committee: Dave Sutton, Mike Passilla, Richard Ingleton, and Nick Heyes for their support and feedback. In addition, Vice Presidents John Moses, Peter Moses, and Larry Goldman made major contributions, as entire sections of this book are derived from their outstanding vision and experience.

We must also thank Executive Editor Sheck Cho and the rest of the John Wiley & Sons team for believing in us, all of our clients for working with us, and everyone who has helped make us a successful company today.

None of this, however, would be possible without the support and commitment of the entire Inforte staff. Their dedication, innovation, and ongoing success have given us the foundation to write this book and leverage our collective experiences.

Finally, Doug would like to thank Michelle, Shawn, Ray and Kathryn Turk, and Dr. Margaret Fleming for all of their support and encouragement.

Philip Bligh and Douglas Turk
Chicago, 2004

A New, More Strategic Approach to CRM

The 1990s saw widespread investment by companies in software applications that automated their sales, service, and marketing processes. As the market for these software applications and services grew, vendors touted the concept of Customer Relationship Management (CRM). CRM was billed as a new business approach designed to centralize customer information, drive deeper customer insight, improve the quality of customer interactions, and encourage a customer-centric business approach. Large businesses were each spending up to $90 million over a three-year period investing in technology, labor, consulting services, and training related to CRM initiatives.[1] In total, companies invested over $2.3 billion in CRM software alone in 2003, and the yearly investment is expected to reach $2.9 billion by 2007.[2] Unfortunately, most initiatives have not paid off because unrealistic expectations, poor linkage of goals to firm strategy, and badly run projects have thwarted the efforts. Organizations focused on technology application implementations rather than the more important business changes required for CRM success. In addition, they did not understand how CRM could strengthen their specific competitive advantages, and instead embarked on expensive efforts to adopt Best Practices embedded within CRM software applications or automate their existing processes regardless of their strategic value. Therefore, most ended up with implementations poorly tailored to their specific competitive needs. As a result, few of those who pursued CRM achieved the goal of significantly improving customer operations, and even fewer gained any competitive advantage in the marketplace.

Grand plans for comprehensive CRM solutions fell by the wayside as firms struggled with project overruns and poor reviews from users. Consequently, many implementations were only partially put to use and some were abandoned altogether. Many CRM software licenses remain unimplemented as companies lost faith in the initiatives, and a significant majority of firms state they have not received an acceptable return on their investment. This is confirmed by the fact that in most cases revenues, customer loyalty, and profits have not risen as a result of CRM.

In view of the hype that accompanied the rise of CRM and the resulting high expectations, many organizations view it as a huge disappointment. This has left many executives confused about what CRM really is and whether they should have invested in it in the first place. Many considered abandoning CRM as a bad or unworkable idea. They asked: Why throw good money after bad?

This is both a shame and a mistake. The ideas and tools provided by CRM are important to efficient operations and—as we will see— powerful tools that help create competitive advantage. At its core, CRM is about pursuing more profitable relationships with customers and any company wishing to succeed must adopt this strategic direction. The key lies in understanding CRM better and the specific way it should be applied to individual businesses. CRM is a business initiative that leverages technology as a tool—not the other way round. Implemented properly, CRM produces lasting gains in revenue and profitability by boosting competitive advantage.

Industry Leaders Show the Way

During our research for this book, we looked extensively for CRM failures and success stories. In Chapter 2, we'll look at the failures in more detail. In looking for success stories, we focused on companies with excellent business results in order to see whether CRM initiatives were actually having positive impacts. Throughout later chapters, we highlight companies that have applied the ideas under the CRM umbrella in ways that are tailored for their individual business and that strengthen their competitive advantages. Leading firms like Zara, Dell Computer, Harrah's, Vanguard, Southwest Airlines, Wal-Mart, Washington Mutual, and Walgreen's have all experienced success with CRM. However, none pursued it in conventional ways. What emerged from our study were clear patterns in how CRM should be approached to achieve lasting returns. We introduce three key approaches in this chapter and cover each in more detail in subsequent chapters:

1. *CRM is not just a technology initiative; it must be approached strategically.*

   When initiated with this perspective, CRM can produce measurable improvements in customer-facing operations in ways that strengthen competitive advantage.

2. *Insight into customers and demand trends should drive CRM agendas.*

   Initial CRM implementations or enhancements to existing CRM infrastructure should be based on adequate information and perspective about customers and the firm's demand environment. Once implemented, CRM should allow organizations to see beyond the boundaries of the internal enterprise, and collect, analyze, and leverage such insight.

3. *CRM must be implemented with an enterprise-wide perspective.*
In practice, many departments of the organization impact customer interactions. CRM can and should help coordinate processes across functional departments and create a cross-departmental mindset in order to deliver tailored treatments to key customer segments.

In the remainder of this chapter we summarize these key lessons, which are covered in more detail in later chapters. But first we must pause to clarify our definition of CRM.

A Clearer Definition of CRM Is Required

A clearer definition of CRM is required to ensure that executives understand its value and for the organization as a whole to assess its proper application. CRM is best described as a three-layered collection of operating philosophy, processes, and technologies that help companies improve their sales, service, and marketing operations. These layers include:

1. The philosophy of organizing the firm in more customer-centric ways, attracting customers, and tailoring service for individual customers or customer segments.

2. Best Practices for managing and integrating sales, service, and marketing processes.

3. Software technologies used to automate and integrate the various sales, service, and marketing processes and activities, and to capture and centralize customer-related information.

A commonly accepted business-oriented definition of CRM from research firm Gartner is as follows:

> Gartner defines CRM as a business strategy that maximizes profitability, revenue and customer satisfaction by organizing around customer segments, fostering behavior that satisfies customers and implementing customer-centric processes. To achieve the long-term value of CRM, enterprises must understand that it is a strategy involving the whole business, and thus should be approached at an enterprise level.[3]

It is important to understand that CRM is both a business approach to improved management of customer operations and a collection of technologies to assist in automating those operations. This is a critical distinction that many early adopters failed to realize. By treating CRM primarily as a technology, they focused only on a secondary aspect and unknowingly reduced the significant strategic value it can deliver.

Before exploring its definition further, it is useful to briefly trace CRM's evolution. CRM began in the early 1990s as a marketer's term for a group of ideas and technologies created to help improve customer-related business practices. It was the logical extension of long-term efforts by companies to keep up with ever changing buyers, markets, and competitors. These challenges intensified with the explosion in the use of PCs and the Internet in the 1990s. The economy surged, everyone had more information at their fingertips, and customer expectations rose rapidly. In response, companies scrambled to deepen knowledge of their individual customers and focus more intensely on the needs of specific customer segments.

At the same time, PC, network, and software architecture evolved to allow cost-effective automation for an increasing number of tasks. Soon, automation of sales force and call center processes transitioned into integrated suites of software that claimed to help manage all customer-related processes and data within the business. Vendors added Internet features and touted the Best Practices embedded in their software. These packages encode Best Practices through the information required for entry on the screens, and the screens flow through the system. The information and screens are also configurable, giving organizations a raft of options in implementing CRM software.

For readers with more limited exposure to CRM, a fuller definition can be given by considering its scope within three categories: Best Practices, Technology Tools, and Strategic Ideas. The following lists some of the key elements of each category.

Best Practices

Best and proven process management and execution guidelines are in key sales, service, and marketing areas. Typically, these practices are gathered as a result of extensive, industry-specific research. Examples include:

- Sales lead management

- Sales territory management

- Pipeline management

- Channel management

- Online sales channel management

- Contract management

- Account and contact management

- Customer service request management

- Field service and dispatch support

- Agreement management

- Call center call routing and management

- Call center service request management

- Online service channel management

- Inventory inquiry

- Direct marketing and campaign management

- Marketing resource management

- Pricing, promotions, and revenue management

- Forecasting and demand management

- Order management

Technology Tools

- *Packaged business applications*

  - *Process automation.* Automation of key activities and processes across sales, service, and marketing: Includes data capture, presentation of all relevant data to business users, and user-inquiry capability.

  - *Embedded Best Practices.* The relevant screen layout, screen-flow, and key data fields associated with the

Best Practices are typically preconfigured in CRM applications. This means that many existing firm processes can be adapted to those implied by the application.

- *Configurability.* Most CRM applications can also be configured or customized to support the firm's proprietary or tailored activities and processes.

- *Workflow.* The flow of customer interactions throughout the enterprise can be closely monitored since most applications provide "workflow" capability. This allows users to track work status and route work to available resources. It also allows alerts to be configured so that operational anomalies—such as a sudden increase in product orders in a certain region—can be immediately flagged.

- *Data storage*

  - Storage of all typical key customer information in secure databases.

  - Storage of customized data fields (such as those generated by proprietary processes).

- *Data inquiry*

  - Ability to easily access and review business information (such as order details, back-orders, inventory availability, logistics schedules, etc.) that is vital to sales, service, and marketing.

- *Performance management tools*

  - Definition of metrics associated with key processes, customers, orders, and so on.

  - Automatic tracking of metrics.

  - Performance reporting capability including customized reports.

- *Analytics*

  - Tools that organize data in ways that allow for fast and flexible querying.

  - Tools that allow analysts to create and change business queries on the fly.

  - Tools that allow data to be quickly sliced, diced, and presented.

As we've seen from the Best Practices and Technology Tools categories, by centralizing customer data and providing a consistent interface for users throughout sales, service, and marketing, CRM can improve service levels through faster and more accurate responses to customers. Also, by providing a more complete picture of current and past customer activity and preferences, CRM improves sales to existing customers. But CRM doesn't stop at simply providing integrated automation of sales, service, and marketing processes. It also recommends additional activities that improve quality and profitability of customer relationships. Examples of these are included within our third category, Strategic Ideas.

Strategic Ideas

- *Customer-centric organizational approaches*

  - *Segmentation.* Approaches for segmenting customers by value and needs and using such distinctions to prioritize and tailor marketing, sales, and service activities throughout the firm.

  - *Tailoring.* Organizational approaches that allow customers to be served in tailored ways, according to their unique needs.

  - *Coordination.* Organizational approaches that allow for different departments to work together much more seamlessly in pursuit of optimal customer service and effectiveness.

- *Improved prospecting and cross-selling*

  - *Targeting.* Methods and tools for targeting attractive customers based on better understanding of valuable segments and their typical needs.

  - *Cross-selling.* Methods and tools for cross-selling based on better understanding of segment needs.

- *Improved visibility into customer profitability*

  - Methods for tracking customer profitability throughout customer life cycles.

  - Approaches for focusing resources on best customer opportunities and dealing with underperforming customers or segments.

- *Return-based marketing*

  - Approaches for growing the value of company brands and assessing brand equity and returns.

  - Approaches for return on investment (ROI)-driven management of marketing initiatives.

- *Customer insight and feedback*

  - Systematic capture of customer and demand information.

  - Systematic feedback of customer and demand information back into each function of the firm.

It is important to recognize that not all CRM elements will fit every company's situation. To find the right solutions for your business, a new and different approach to CRM is required.

Three Lessons from Leaders

Based on the successful methods of industry leaders, we recommend three key approaches to successful CRM. Or better stated, we offer guidelines that will identify and help implement business improvements that enhance customer value while strengthening profits and strategy. This section outlines these approaches and Chapters 3 through 6 cover them in more detail.

CRM Must Be Approached Strategically and Linked to Clear Business Gains

A major element of past failures has been the tendency to implement CRM ideas and technologies without first identifying the firm's key

13

levers of competitive advantage. Higher prices, improved market share, or cost advantages over rivals produce the big gains, and achieving these typically means finding new and unique ways to deliver value to customers. In failing to tie CRM to their sources of advantage, investments and efforts have been diluted across lower return activities. Other activities might produce efficiency gains, but not deliver enduring gains over rivals. For example, many firms decided to convert all current business processes and activities to Best Practices recommended in the CRM software packages and use the packages to automate them. Others decided to keep existing processes the way they were and spent millions of dollars customizing the CRM application to automate them. Such significant investments in the automation of existing processes might be appropriate if the processes concerned were critical to the firm's strategic advantages, but little consideration was given to this. The key is to realize that only certain CRM components will produce worthwhile gains. Best Practices, after all, are by definition the same practices used by rivals.

The organization must determine which Best Practices, proprietary processes, and technologies are absolutely necessary in order to avoid competitive disadvantage, while focusing the majority of time and attention on Strategic Ideas, strengthening processes and technologies that help bolster the firm's competitive advantages. To be sure, certain business processes do not provide an advantage and *should* be standardized and automated. Not doing this can lead to serious disadvantage. But too much focus on Best Practices distracts from efforts to strengthen advantages and blurs the firm's distinctiveness in the marketplace. CRM must be implemented in this tailored manner to truly help improve value for customers, strengthen competitive position, and boost business performance. The new approach first determines the distinctive activities within the firm's value chain before creating agendas and committing investments to CRM.

To illustrate the strategic approach to CRM, consider the following examples. In 2002, in order to reduce customer wait times, Southwest Airlines adopted an automated system that replaced its hallmark plastic boarding cards with paper boarding passes printed at the ticket counter, skycap counter, or boarding gate. Not only does this improve gate efficiency, it also improved customer satisfaction by eliminating yet one more line customers had to endure at the airport.[4] At first glance, this does not seem like CRM, and certainly it is unlike the approaches taken by most companies in the past. But this is an excellent example of an improvement that increases customer satisfaction (by reducing wait times at airports) and reinforces the firm's low-price positioning by speeding up (and lowering the cost of) gate turnaround. This is the type of clear benefit CRM must have. Most successful companies viewed CRM as a series of similar initiatives aimed at improving areas of sales, service, and marketing. Unlike unsuccessful CRM users, they did not pursue large blanket initiatives with unclear business goals. Similarly, Walgreen's provided faster and more flexible buying options for customers by adding an online pharmacy[5] that strengthened the company's core value proposition of convenience for the customer. In each case, these improvements increased customer value, but in ways designed to strengthen the company's strategic value proposition.

These are the types of CRM efforts leading companies have undertaken. They are specific and tailored, often relatively small and focused initiatives, which are designed to systematically strengthen the firm's marketplace advantages. At Southwest and Walgreen's they are respectively making plane tickets cheaper, and shopping more convenient. This is a common pattern among the leading firms; they never forget what creates competitive advantage in the marketplace and why customers buy from them. They have not pursued big CRM programs with lofty and vague goals. Instead, they are on a continuous quest for ideas that strengthen their core value proposition. The winning companies have a clear mission and follow a step-by-step approach in achieving it. Each idea for improving value for customers is tested against three critical questions:

1. What is the value being added and for which customers?

2. Does it strengthen or dilute the firm's strategy?

3. What is the resulting affect on firm profitability?

By pursuing improvements that satisfy these criteria, customer value is enhanced, profitability is improved, and the firm's competitive position is strengthened. This is a straightforward customer-first approach to improving your business. It is simply cheaper, quicker, and more effective than the popular but failed technology-first CRM approaches of the past.

As mentioned, CRM initiatives have not strengthened their sources of competitive advantage for most companies. In some cases, CRM has actually been harmful as effort and funds are expended on the wrong improvements for the wrong customers. A clear understanding of the firm's strategy and sources of competitive advantage must be the starting point for each initiative.

Using Harvard professor Michael Porter's strategy frameworks and research, we show how top-performing companies are focused on a core value proposition and then hard wire the value proposition into every policy, process, and behavior throughout the firm. For example, Southwest is the low-fare, no-frills airline, and every aspect of their business is based on supporting this strategy. They fly mostly short routes between less-congested airports, using only one type of airplane. They don't serve food or offer higher classes of service. For Southwest, CRM is primarily about looking for improvements that keep prices low for their customers. They invest in systems that reduce gate time and get planes into the air faster, and they avoid overly sophisticated frequent-flier programs that don't benefit their core-customer base of leisure fliers. Southwest marches to its own beat and pursues improvements in customer operations differently than other airlines.[6]

Producing enduring top- and bottom-line gains requires understanding your strategic advantages and working continuously to strengthen them. Great companies approach CRM primarily by using it to strengthen their unique advantages in the marketplace. By identifying the sources of competitive advantage and how they are manifested in the policies, processes, and behaviors within the firm, clear guidelines emerge that identify what types of CRM initiatives a firm should be pursuing.

Insight into Customers and Demand Patterns Should Drive the CRM Agenda

In maximizing the benefits of CRM, the firm's strategy defines the playing field, but customer insights define the plays. Customer tastes, habits, and expectations evolve rapidly, and meeting these changing needs requires a formal approach to capturing insight into customers

17

and patterns of demand. But we must first look at CRM from the customers' individual perspectives to truly understand how each of them is different, and we must better understand the reasons for a customer's purchase. We must ask: How do they put our product or service to use? Once this information is acquired it is possible to identify opportunities that create meaningful value for customers. At Wal-Mart, ongoing customer-insight efforts generate ideas for new products and services. For example, the finding that 50 percent of women shoppers have an undeveloped roll of film in their purse led to the creation of an in-store, half-hour film processing service.[7]

For leading companies, CRM improvements tend to be customer-segment specific, due to the differences in needs and value of each segment. Understanding the profit potential of each segment helps prioritize efforts. Gaining customer insights is a continuing process requiring formal methods for gathering feedback and translating that information into action.

In conjunction with gaining the customer's perspective, changes in the marketplace and the nature of demand must be captured systematically. Top-performing companies are in-tune with the types and levels of customer demand and are highly responsive to this information. High visibility into demand is the operational linchpin of successful companies. Virtually all critical planning decisions—from parts ordering to defining marketing campaigns, to hiring and budgeting—are driven by forecasted revenue levels. The level, type, and timing of demand are the critical pieces of the decision-making puzzle. Accurate forecasting must be followed up by cross-department planning processes designed to align each area of the firm to emerging market realities.

Despite the importance of demand visibility, most companies are poor forecasters. This deficiency dooms them to subpar results regardless of the strength of their strategies. Conventional wisdom tells them that forecasting is impossible to get right and so they don't focus on improving it. Yet the companies that forecast successfully produce consistent results and avoid nasty earnings and cash flow surprises. By avoiding the distractions of ugly surprises, they can focus completely on increasing value and strengthening their advantages over competitors.

At Wal-Mart, for example, demand sensitivity is a high priority. They have invested millions in the RetailLink systems that communicate a rolling two years of sales data to all suppliers on a weekly basis. This data allows suppliers to use simple statistical tools to project upcoming sales.[8] In another example, Dell has built electronic links with suppliers to communicate replenishment needs, in some partnerships, on an *hourly* basis. In addition, forecasting is a vital part of the job for Dell's entire sales force. They are trained in how to walk customers through standard questions and identify critical business events that are likely to trigger sales.[9]

Good revenue projections and coordinated internal reaction allows leading firms to focus time and attention on struggling business units, product lines, or markets, while also exploiting opportunities derived from emerging customer demand more effectively. These activities create a virtuous circle. Early warning avoids wasting time on firefighting caused by missed earnings and cash-flow problems while timely alerts free up resources for capitalizing on opportunities which have become clearer by way of the improved visibility.

A demand-driven operating philosophy goes hand in hand with our new strategic approach to CRM. In tandem, they will deliver on the original promise of CRM: significant revenue gains, improved profitability, and stronger, more lucrative customer relationships.

An Enterprise-Wide Approach to Managing Customers Is Essential

Strategic focus and customer insights enable a firm to create distinctive ways to treat each customer or customer segment. This leads to more intelligent targeting of prospects and enhanced value delivered to customers. Customer interactions should be defined based on these specific needs and attributes. Therefore, each function of the firm should organize in ways that allow rapid response to the needs of individual customers and customer segments. Differential treatment of customers allows a company to prioritize investment and resources to ensure focus on the most valuable customer opportunities.

Every function of the firm impacts customers in some way, but too often these influences are not coordinated across the firm. A company-wide plan is required to define organizational approach, policies, and processes that deliver unique services to each customer or segment. Traditionally, firms have created functional strategies that define the policies, processes, and plans for each of its functional areas. But formal plans for coordinating customer-specific treatments across the enterprise have been virtually nonexistent. A formal enterprise-wide approach to customer interactions enables the coordination of every policy, process, and function, and delivers differentiated treatment to customers at consistent quality levels.

The three key lessons derived from industry leaders can serve as guidelines that allow every company to think about CRM in ways that improve profitability and competitive advantage. In Chapters 3 through 6 we show how to tie CRM to company strategy, implement customer and demand insight processes, and define an enterprise-wide approach to customer interactions. The final chapter provides implementation guidelines showing how organizations can get started on the journey to strategic CRM.

Key Points

- Most companies lost sight of the original goals of CRM: to attract, retain, and serve customers in ways that achieve enduring increases in top- and bottom-line performance.

- Companies implemented CRM without properly tying its goals to their unique strategies. This approach results only in modest operational gains that are similar to those gained by rivals and does not improve competitive advantage.

- Three key lessons emerge from a study of how successful companies approached CRM:

  1. CRM must be implemented strategically with clear business goals.

  2. CRM agendas should be driven by insight into customers and demand patterns.

  3. An enterprise-wide approach to customer management is required to coordinate tailored treatment of customers based on their value and needs.

Notes

1. Intellibusiness, "Market Size Insights," *www.intellibusiness.com/c2c/fc/market-stats-c2c-01.htm*, available as of January 28, 2004.

2. Tom Topolinski, "Predicts 2004: The CRM Software Market Is Recovering," Stamford: Gartner, *www.gartner.com*, available as of December 8, 2003.

3. Scott D. Nelson, "Management Update: The Eight Building Blocks of CRM," Stamford: Gartner, *www2.cio.com/analyst/report1483.html*, available as of June 19, 2003.

4. Southwest Airlines, "New Southwest Airlines Boarding System Saves Time at the Airport; Automated Boarding Pass Allows Single-Stop Check-in," Company Press Release, June 17, 2002.

5. Jim Collins, *Good to Great: Why Some Companies Make the Leap, and Others Don't*. New York: HarperBusiness, October 2001.

6. James L. Heskett and Roger Hallowell, "Southwest Airlines—1993 (A)," *Harvard Business Review*, #694023. Boston: Harvard Business School Press, August 1, 2001.

7. Jerry Useem, "America's Most Admired Companies: One Nation under Wal-Mart," *FORTUNE*. New York: Time Inc., February 18, 2003.

8. Tom Smith, "Consumer Products Company Builds Adhesive Supply Chain Relationships," *InternetWeek*, *www.internetweek.com/story/showArticle.jhtml?articleID=6405960*, available as of March 1, 2002.

9. Michael Dell and Joan Magretta, "The Power of Virtual Integration: An Interview with Dell Computer's Michael Dell," *Harvard Business Review*, #98208. Boston: Harvard Business School Press, March/April 1998.

CHAPTER 2

A Review of CRM Failures

CRM is expected to remain an important part of the commercial and government landscape, with projections of 9 percent CAGR between 2003 and 2007.[1] In addition, government agencies are rapidly adopting and adapting commercial CRM ideas. The entire annual CRM market is expected to reach $14.5 billion in 2007, compared to $9.6 billion in 2002.[2] As an executive at a large insurer put it:

> CRM is a very important business solution. Our [customers] want better tools and capabilities and product options, and they're driving us into this space. But there's a heavy risk involved. How you connect CRM to the back office and bring customers on board makes all the difference. When you stumble, the very credibility of your company is at stake.[3]

Indeed, while CRM is expected to grow, shortfalls in returns are expected to continue. Recent industry research shows that only 16 percent of CRM projects provide real, reportable business return on investment (ROI).[4] In a related study, of the 43 percent of respondents who claimed to have achieved success in their CRM projects, only half of this group was able to cite solid details about returns. An estimated 12 percent of projects fail to go live at all.[5]

Clearly, CRM remains a vital yet risky enterprise, with success riding on organizations correctly approaching its planning and implementation.

The remainder of this book is dedicated to providing background and guideposts needed to forge a workable approach to CRM. But first, it is instructive for executives and teams to understand what types of failures occurred in the past, why, and their business impact. Knowing the pitfalls will help firms understand the need for a new approach and improves the probability of capturing the opportunity CRM represents.

CRM failures have been costly, disruptive, and embarrassing. Red ink, shareholder losses, upset customers, lost market share, lawsuits, and career setbacks are all typical outcomes of CRM failures. Several such failures have been publicly documented as companies have cited CRM problems for performance shortfalls during earnings announcements. In this chapter, we have collected some of these stories. Obviously, few companies are willing to detail failed initiatives but the information available provides strong indications of patterns of failure. In addition, the authors have personally seen the aftermath of many situations where initiatives had gone awry and these experiences, together with the documented failures, provide an eye-opening dossier of reasons for failure. Ultimately, the mistakes of the past will help to set the proper expectations and goals for the future.

What Went Wrong with CRM

In January 2002, Philadelphia-based CIGNA HealthCare migrated 3.5 million of its members to new claims processing and customer service processes and systems.[6] The broad-based $1 billion initiative included CRM and an overhaul of its legacy technology infrastructure. Benefits did not materialize as planned and resulting impacts on customer service caused the nation's fourth largest insurer to lose 6 percent of its health-care membership in 2002.

CIGNA wanted integrated processes and systems for enrollment, eligibility, and claims processing so that customers would get one bill, medical claims could be processed faster and more efficiently, and customer service reps would have a single unified view of members. This meant consolidating complex back-end processes and systems for claims processing and billing, and integrating them with new CRM applications on the front-end. The project required complex technical work and an overhaul of the way business processes work together between front and back office as well as an overhaul of customer service staffing levels and skills. In addition, new processes and applications were designed to allow members to enroll, check the status of their claims and benefits, and choose from different health-plan offerings—all online.

There are several reasons why CIGNA was under considerable pressure to make these changes. First, along with other insurers such as Aetna and Humana, they were being sued by thousands of doctors about payment delays. They were also being accused of deliberately rejecting or delaying payments to save money. (CIGNA recently settled most of the doctors' lawsuits by pledging faster and more accurate claims processing with the new integrated platforms and promising to pay millions to physicians in compensation.) In 2001, Georgia's insurance commissioner found serious issues with CIGNA's claims processing system and it was fined by the state of Georgia. CIGNA signed a consent order pledging to reform its claims processing system.

Also, during sales cycles, CIGNA had promised large employee accounts that it would have revamped systems for improving customer service up and running by early 2002. Finally, the company had reported disappointing second quarter results in 2001 and was under pressure to cut costs. Although some selective hiring of staff was planned in order to alter the firm's skills mix, the goal was a net reduction of staff by 2,000 people through layoffs.

At first, CIGNA conducted small scale migrations, moving its members in small groups of approximately 10,000 people at a time. During this time, problems were limited and manageable. At the same time, the customer service areas were being revamped in anticipation of the new-fangled systems. Huge gains in claims processing and customer service efficiency were expected, and the company started laying off reps as part of a consolidation of service centers. In 2002, the company terminated 3,100 employees and spent $33 million in severance payments. CIGNA also invested $32 million in the new regional service centers.

At this point, in January 2002, with members renewing and new members lining up, the company performed a mass migration to the new infrastructure. Serious problems emerged immediately. Members had trouble obtaining, confirming, and inquiring about coverage. Employees at one member company effectively lost coverage due to membership data problems. Member ID cards were issued with incorrect numbers and prescription icons. Some people could not get their prescriptions filled at drugstores.

As a result, a flurry of inquiries put CIGNA's new customer service operation to the test. But lower staff levels left the centers short-handed. Customers who phoned were put on hold, and when they did get through, some of the new reps struggled to navigate the new systems.

In addition, data from back-end systems did not show up properly in the customer service systems, making it difficult for reps to fully understand the customer's situation.

In the rush to go live, the system's ability to handle claims and service from front to back and in large volumes was not adequately tested. Problems in one area cascaded into others; staffing levels were inadequate, and staff were improperly prepared. Rather than realize that benefits would come over time as the company became used to new processes and systems, they expected them the day the switches were flipped.

Given this experience, CIGNA has now slowed down the pace of migration and solidified the processes, systems, and staffing. It also has improved testing practices. By mid-2002, CIGNA was moving new members without major problems. In January 2003, it successfully performed a significant migration of 700,000 members. It also successfully launched *www.MyCIGNA.com*, a website for members to look up their benefits, select health plans, check claim status, search for health information, and communicate with nurses online.

Now that the problems have been handled, the company is processing medical claims more efficiently and servicing customers better than in the past. Some of the initiative's original goals have now been achieved. The elimination of duplication in claims processing and billing, as well as other benefits, have allowed the company to streamline its sales force and medical management team. However, the price tag for the project has exceeded the $1 billion planned and significant damage was done to the company's reputation and its financial performance.

CRM Contributes to a Scary Halloween for Hershey

Candy producers record 40 percent of their annual sales between October and December. Halloween, the biggest candy-consuming holiday, accounts for about $2 billion in sales.[7] For a candy producer, missing Halloween is like a toy company missing Christmas. Unfortunately, in 1999, that's just what happened to Hershey, the nation's largest candy maker.[8] Just before the big candy season, shelves at warehouses and retailers lay empty of treats such as Hershey bars, Reese's Peanut Butter Cups, Kisses, Kit-Kats, and Rolos. Though inventory was plentiful, orders had not arrived and distributors could not fully supply their retailers.

Hershey announced in September that it would miss its third-quarter earnings forecasts due to problems with new customer order and delivery systems that had been recently rolled out. The new enterprise resource planning (ERP) and CRM processes and technology implemented earlier in the year had affected Hershey's ability to take orders and deliver product. The $112 million system aimed to modernize business practices and provide front-to-back automation from order-taking to truck-loading, but Hershey lost market share as problems allowed rivals to benefit during the season. Mars and Nestlé both reported unusual spurts of late orders as the Halloween season grew nearer. The most frustrating aspect of the situation is that Hershey had plenty of candy on hand to fill all its orders. It just couldn't deliver the orders to customers.

By December 1999, the company announced it would miss already lowered earnings targets. It stated that lower demand in the last few months of the year was in part a consequence of the earlier fulfillment and service issues.

Hershey had embarked on the project in 1996 to better coordinate deliveries with its retailers, allowing it to keep its inventory costs under control. The company also needed to address Y2K problems with its legacy systems. CRM, ERP, and supply chain management systems were implemented, along with 5,000 personal computers and a complex network of servers. The intention was to integrate these software and hardware components in order to let the 1,200-person sales force shepherd orders step-by-step through the distribution process. Sales could also better coordinate with other departments to handle every issue from order placement to final delivery. The system was also designed to help Hershey measure promotional campaigns and set prices, plus help run the company's accounting operations, track ingredients, and schedule production and truck loading.

Hershey realized that the business process changes involved with such a transformation were highly intricate. However, despite the size and complexity of the undertaking, the firm decided on an aggressive implementation plan that entailed a large piece of the new infrastructure going live at the same time. Unfortunately, the project ran behind schedule and wasn't ready until July 1999 when the Halloween orders had already begun to come in. Problems in getting customer orders into the system and transmitting the correct details of those orders to warehouses for shipping began immediately. By August, the company was 15 days behind in filling orders, and in September, order turnaround time was twice as long as usual.

In recent years, Hershey sales growth had exceeded its rivals, and the company was expecting 4 to 6 percent growth that year. However, sales instead slipped and the company admitted that problems with the new system alone had reduced sales by $100 million during the period.

In the past few years, other companies have experienced similar CRM-related problems. For example, printer manufacturer Lexmark abandoned a CRM initiative in 2002 and announced that it would take a charge of $15.8 million.[9] Similarly, Agilent Technologies blamed its quarterly profit shortfall in August 2002 on problems installing a new company-wide software system.[10] Separately, Carsdirect.com estimated in a lawsuit that it suffered $50 million in operating losses due its inability to adequately meet customer demand after installing customer-tracking tools.[11]

The cost of CRM failure is dramatic and can take its toll in many areas of the business. The following summarizes the typical impacts by category:

Financial Performance

- Market share and operating losses
- Failure to achieve a return on investments
- Budget overruns
- High post-implementation running costs

Customer Service Quality

- Customer confusion, frustration, and dissatisfaction
- Lower service levels
- Slower time to market
- Negative brand perception

Sales Effectiveness

- Lower sales force productivity

- Increased sales force cynicism toward new systems

- Increased sales force turnover

Cultural Impacts

- Low morale within IT and affected departments

- Growing cultural cynicism within the company toward adopting business change

- Company-wide loss of confidence in its ability to enact change

- Lost jobs in the executive suite

- Propensity for companies to become overly conservative with regard to investments in strategic initiatives. This leads to dampened innovation, a failure to strengthen advantages, and deferring the update of aging processes and infrastructure

Why CRM Projects Fail

Because it changes the way a company interacts with customers and the daily jobs of thousands of people throughout the organization, there are many potential failure points for CRM. These implementations are strategic in nature, change policy and business practices,

Exhibit 2.1
Leading CRM Risk Factors

(% citing risk in top 3)

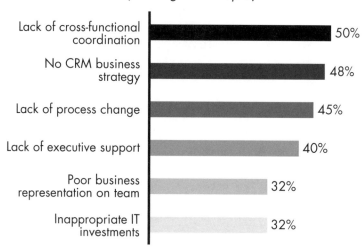

Source: Meta Group, *Leadership Strategies in CRM,* January 2000; Data Warehousing Institute (March 2001).

and require the entire organization to coordinate closely toward specific goals. Exhibit 2.1 demonstrates the most commonly cited reasons for failure.

Like all complex initiatives, risk exists and must be managed. The following section describes the most common reasons for failure using broadly defined categories:

- Poor objective setting

- Lack of senior leadership

- Inadequate planning and scope setting

- Implementation missteps

- Lack of change management

- Inadequate post-implementation operation

Poor Objective Setting

These failures relate to the overall aims of the initiative. In many ways, these are the most common cause of CRM failures, as poorly defined goals complicate downstream efforts and undermine end results.

Failing to Align Initiative with Strategy

As introduced in Chapter 1 and covered in more detail in the next chapter, CRM initiatives must be properly aligned to firm strategy. Unfortunately, most initiatives tend to be based solely on gains in efficiency and do not produce any competitive advantage. Little consideration is typically given to how the goals of the CRM initiative will help bolster the firm's unique competitive advantages in the marketplace. As a result, arduous and expensive efforts result only in minor efficiency gains that come after the big changes initially slow the company down. The overwhelming majority of companies fail to align goals to strategy, so much so that it is a rarity for a CRM initiative to begin with a discussion of the firm's competitive advantages in the marketplace.

In one case, a financial products and services company spent over $10 million on efforts to duplicate its highly complex customer-specific contract process. This required significant modification to a software package that didn't support such processes out of the box. Eventually the process was halted as senior management became aware that the program was not helping address its more fundamental

35

issues—the obsolescence of certain product lines and the need to diversify into new markets.

Failing to Anchor the Initiative

Planning and implementing CRM projects is a difficult job requiring experienced program managers capable of shepherding through policy, processes, people, and technology change while keeping all branches of an organization, several teams, and multiple vendors in concert. We have observed that successful initiatives tend to be anchored firmly in the objectives they follow. For example, they are either focused on making select strategic changes, re-platforming existing processes, or converting current processes to Best Practices (often those found in purchased software packages). Some successful programs contain a combination of all three, but most are more focused. Exhibit 2.2 describes this anchoring.

Without clarity around the type of goals being pursued, the program will default to a hodge-podge of all three objectives. In this unsatisfactory situation, few within the organization agree on the goals. Without alignment and a strong guiding light, decision making is difficult, compromises are rife, and initiatives tend to limp across the finish line late and without fully satisfying any of the stakeholders.

Focusing on Internal rather than Customer Priorities

In pursuing CRM, many organizations focus on existing customer processes rather than enhancing or building new interactions that customers may prefer. They typically fail to spend enough time critically evaluating their current operations from the customer's perspective, and this inside-out thinking can cause significant misfires.

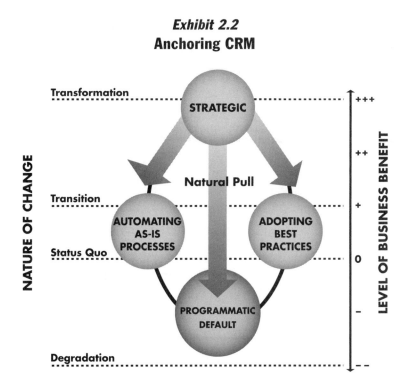

Exhibit 2.2
Anchoring CRM

For example, General Motors Acceptance Corp.'s commercial-mortgage operation (GMACCM) managed to unduly upset customers during its CRM implementation in 1999.[12] GMACCM, which is an industry leader and known for its technological prowess, implemented an automated voice-response technology as the first point of contact with commercial loan customers inquiring about their loan balances and other information. But upon activation the company found that commercial customers simply weren't willing to spend time punching in numbers and navigating the system. Literally 99 percent of its 20,000 customers were calling the 800 number and zeroing out to a customer service "operator". Customers were annoyed, complaints were up, and loan officers were losing business. Rivals used this misstep as a marketing tool to lure customers away.

In another example, Owens Corning began a CRM implementation project in 1992.[13] The company had acquired a number of smaller companies to expand beyond its core insulation product lines, which led to many pockets of unconsolidated electronic customer records. In addition, marketing approaches weren't consistent across the many parts of the organization. On top of this, the company was getting its internal processes updated and automated using a large ERP package which siphoned budget and attention away from the CRM effort and made it difficult for the CRM teams to create new types of interactions for customers. The over-emphasis on internal priorities bogged Owens Corning down, preventing vital customer-facing changes. Owens has stated that a better approach would have been to start with the customer wants and needs and work backward.

In case after case, poor results clearly illustrate the importance of gaining the customer's perspective up front. Objectives cannot be appropriately set unless the outside-in perspective has been attained.

Lack of Senior Leadership

In many organizations, top management is either not engaged at all, loses interest once the initial high-level decisions have been made, or doesn't focus long enough to ensure successful post-implementation operation. These kinds of leadership shortfalls sound the death knell for CRM initiatives.

Leaders Fail to Engage

BMC, the $1.5 billion software company, was an early CRM visionary and rode out two failed CRM initiatives before achieving success and

returns. In the first attempt, processes and systems were implemented without the involvement of key executives or business units. The
new system suffered from very low utilization, with only 30 to 50
percent of users adopting it. The system was also plagued by problems caused by inaccurate data. The second attempt went forward
under the mistaken impression that all the users needed to get
onboard were more features and better data. The system again failed
to capture wide usage.

BMC's persistence paid off on attempt number three once they
realized the need for executive support. The project team obtained
C-suite commitment and formed a steering committee of IT and
business owners. In addition, more than 150 grass-roots–level salespeople helped define the system's features and usability and this time
adoption soared to 97 percent.[14] BMC spent more than $10 million
on the third effort alone, but returns are expected to be in the order
of $70 million the next two to three years as sales reps increase their
leads and convert more of them to sales.

Another common leadership engagement issue is a tendency for
newly hired executives to be unsupportive of current or past CRM
initiatives. Often, these leaders have their own ideas on how things
need to be done. In most cases, however, this spreads confusion and
creates apathy or active opposition to the program. Risk of failure is
significantly increased as a result.

Leaders Disengage before Mission Is Accomplished

Even after high-level planning and approval is achieved, senior executives must stay with the program through completion and beyond.
Executives often lose interest once the project is underway, but teams

can easily lose control, and the various areas of the firm can quickly become unaligned. Another problem is that after implementation, companies often forget to carry out measurement procedures to assess how the initiative is performing. They also fail to tie employee and management compensation plans to the goals and results of the initiative. By engaging leaders at every stage, the majority of common risks and failings can be closely monitored and mitigated.

Inadequate Planning and Scope Setting

After objectives have been set, firms often stumble at the critical planning stage. Attempting too much, not addressing vital changes to business processes, and not removing organizational roadblocks are typical failings.

Attempting "Big Bang" Implementations

As the CIGNA and Hershey examples illustrate, companies tend to bite off more than they can chew or digest. Large initiatives are more complex and have higher failure rates. Unfortunately, companies tend to try satisfying the needs of too many areas of the firm with each initiative, causing scope to become bloated in a "boil the ocean" approach to CRM. In an example of tackling too large a task, monster.com rolled out a new sales application intended to enable the growth of the company's orders and revenue. Unfortunately, the system was over-configured with too many features and its performance so slow that the inside sales representatives were unable to use it. In addition, the field sales force was unable to access their accounts and customer information for a full year. The company admits that it underestimated the complexity of the effort.

In another example, Dow Chemical attempted a large scale CRM rollout to its global salesforce in 1996.[15] But business processes were not adequately defined and the tool failed to adequately support remote users. This first, overly-complex initiative failed, but later, small localized CRM initiatives started to emerge throughout the firm. These implementations were highly focused and much smaller in scope. They allowed Dow Chemical to more effectively address specific issues and the size of projects allowed for better visibility, control over investment, and higher success rates.

A more incremental approach to CRM implementation is much easier to manage, but many organizations shy away from this, fearing the political difficulties of prioritizing scope and delaying benefits for various parties. An incremental approach also makes achieving buy-in throughout the firm more difficult, but avoids the disastrous costs of widespread operational problems. Exhibit 2.3 demonstrates the increase in risk as initiatives grow larger.

Failing to Adequately Address Business Process

Recently, a large telecom company rolled out a $7 million software package to help improve its customer segmentation and marketing approaches. Though the firm provided sales and marketers with a tool, they failed to identify and enact the new policies and processes needed to put the tool to proper use. As a result, few benefits were gained.

In all surveys of CRM project successes and failures, lack of time and attention to business processes is one of the most common complaints. Processes define the sequence of events and help identify the information passed from one person or department to another. If new tools enable new tasks or alter existing ones, the impact on business

Exhibit 2.3
Assessing CRM Project Risk

INITIATIVE SIZE,
Function Points (FP)

AVERAGE DURATION OF PROJECT, months

	Probable Outcomes, %				Examples:
100	81	12	7	9	1	• Insurance Administration process & system = 15,000 FP
1,000	62	18	20	22	8	• "Big-Bang" CRM initiative = 10,000 – 100,000 FP
10,000	28	24	48	36	14	
100,000	14	21	65	48	26	

On-time or early — Delayed — Stopped

Expected duration — Deviation at completion

Source: Capers Jones, *Patterns of Software System Failure and Success*, London: International Tomson Computer Press, 1996; McKinsey analysis.

process needs to be defined up front. Even if the users of the tools understand the reasons for a change in their procedures, the people in neighboring departments might not.

Another common failure in defining scope for initiatives is a tendency to automate current practices without addressing the redundancies, outmoded practices, and other problems that become ingrained in business processes over time. In migrating to a new system, business users tend to fixate on not losing any current functionality. Yet few spend enough time objectively assessing how valuable current functionality really is. At a leading regional bank, $16 million was invested in licenses for a leading packaged application. The firm then customized the solution to the point where it looked like the home-grown system they were trying to replace. It then rolled the solution out to 3000 users, but the adoption was extremely poor. Other than when monthly sales pipeline reports were due, fewer than 1 percent of users logged in to the system. This false start cost the company at least $13 million as the initiative was substantially reworked.

The following process failings are typical:

- *Perpetuating existing process flaws.*

   Duplicating current processes in new software packages without addressing flaws, outmoded practices, or redundancies in current processes.

- *Over-investing in nonstrategic processes.*

   Spending too much effort on reautomating or improving practices that do not provide competitive advantage (see Chapter 3 for a discussion of competitive advantage versus operational effectiveness). This can result in over-customization of the CRM tools, leading to technical complexity, buggy software, poor usability, and poor performance. By the same token, over-investing in the wrong areas also results in a lack of attention to strengthening the processes that do provide advantages.

- *Overwriting unique processes.*

   Undermining the firm's advantages by overwriting important proprietary processes with generic Best Practices.

- *Failing to update processes.*

   Failing to update key processes to reflect the implementation of new tools.

During its successful third attempt, BMC realized that revamping current processes was crucial to getting the best from their CRM tools.

New tools can be very difficult to use effectively if old processes remain untouched. As a user at BMC remarked before the processes were addressed and fixed, using the tool was like driving a car with the steering wheel set on the wrong side.

Allowing Internal Structure and Politics to Impact Customer Experience

Organizations often fail to realize the extent to which their internal structure affects customer experience. Customers are often frustrated as they attempt to navigate the customer service department, or scratch their heads about why it takes so long for requests to work their way through the organization. One of the goals of CRM is to improve enterprise-wide coordination to benefit customers, but often, well-designed front-end customer interactions are foiled behind the scenes by the old ways of doing things.

At GMACCM, the internal structure of the customer service department had been traditionally divided along functional lines. This meant, for example, that different parts of the department dealt with loan origination versus loan servicing. When CRM was first rolled out, customers were "expected" to know GMACCM's internal structure and nomenclature well enough to know what department to request. Of course, not many callers did, and legitimate customer frustration resulted.[16]

Implementation Missteps

Even well-planned CRM implementations are complex and myriad issues and problems can ensue. Many are common to the complexities of managing any major initiative, including following a proven methodology, risk analysis and mitigation, scope creep, and sound schedule and budget management. This section highlights two particular challenges common to CRM implementations:

1. Improperly staffed teams, and

2. Falling into technology traps

Improperly Staffed Teams

Most organizations staff teams with too many technical people and not enough business users. To illustrate the point, BMC went from engaging a handful of business users in its first two CRM attempts, to actively leveraging over 150 business users in its successful third attempt.

Without well-balanced teams, tasks can't be achieved in the project's time frame and decisions are skewed. Teams must have balanced skills across functional and business processes, technical integration, and change management capabilities to mitigate this risk.

Even when business users are involved, teams can remain poorly balanced across business areas. Teams can become dominated by one particular user group or business area—typically an original sponsor of the initiative or the most active participants in the implementation. By paying greater attention to the initiative, an executive from a particular area might unduly influence project decisions. The executive might even start reprioritizing goals to their advantage or steamrolling the project manager into decisions that stretch resources. Since CRM initiatives require so much interaction, personal relationships can override sound decision making. It can be difficult for project managers to keep a tight enough rein on the situation and in many cases resulting decisions will not align well with the firm's original goals for the initiative.

Falling into Technology Traps

Although technology itself is typically not the most common cause of failure, its complexity requires projects to be carefully planned and properly budgeted and staffed. In addition, delays in policy, process, and organizational decisions can cause teams to rush through vital engineering and technology tasks. In many cases, technology teams are forced to make assumptions about system functionality due to long delays in business decisions. Mistakes require time-consuming rework or cause disconnects between how business and technology staff believe the system should be working.

In addition, IT-led projects tend to over-engineer the solutions as the role of technology is overemphasized. Similarly, many IT teams will spend too much time tinkering with new technology components. Unfortunately, brand new hardware is often being unwrapped in the IT department before the team has finished defining the initiative and the proverbial cart leaves the gate before the horse.

In general, technology issues tend to arise when:

- Using new and untested technologies in critical situations

- Not dedicating enough testing time to the technology implementation

- Failing to spend enough time understanding, gathering, and preparing company data

- Underestimating the complexity and cost of integrating one technology system with another

- Over-customizing CRM tools, leading to installations that are buggy and slow

Lack of Change Management

CRM initiatives significantly impact jobs, roles, skills, and the daily routine of an organization, and are often disruptive and initially unpopular among the rank and file. The people aspects of large initiatives are often the most challenging part, with politics and organizational conflicts being the norm in CRM initiatives. Without adequate preparation, employees and even entire departments will be apathetic or even hostile to the change. Yet many organizations fail to assign time in their plans to prepare for and deal with the change. In fact, change management is often the first item struck from proposed plans and budgets. Executives who have bought into the initiative may assume that employees are as excited as they are and face a rude awakening when confronted with opposition. An executive at Mutual of Omaha relates how the CRM initiative was announced to an employee meeting and was greeted with a sea of rolling eyes. It prompted executives to immediately increase efforts to help the organization prepare for and cope with the change.[17]

Another common CRM problem relates to the structure of most modern corporations. For example, most businesses are structured to have a corporate head office and subordinate business units—each of which has a degree of autonomy. The problem is that many firms try to dictate CRM initiatives to business units, despite the fact that each typically has its own unique competitive strategy. Many companies try to adopt a single software package as an enterprise standard which allows them to purchase licenses in bulk at lower prices. This may make good financial sense but it forces each business unit to use the corporate standard CRM tool, and one size typically does not fit all when it comes to CRM. Some standard packages are overkill for the needs of certain businesses and each business has competitive advantages they are trying to create or strengthen. Shoehorning every business unit into one package is a serious failing. Executives at the business units find their goals compromised and often fight against adopting the standard-issue software. This strains relations between the corporate and business unit entities and increases the already complex task of delivering on the CRM opportunity.

If a company successfully generates excitement for a CRM initiative, this can create another problem—inflated expectations. There are countless cases where the team has brought the initiative in on time only to find user or executive expectations were very different. Executives wonder why they spent the money and business users fail to see the benefit of adopting the changes.

Inadequate Post-Implementation Operation

CRM is an ongoing process not an event. It must be carefully managed over time, even after a successful rollout. Even if excellent user adoption is at first achieved, success will fade if CRM is not nurtured. The results of new approaches and tool usage must be tracked and reviewed regularly by management. The company must invest over time in upgrades to process and technology. These will not be trivial and some may require careful managing. For example, AT&T Wireless recently announced that three million users had trouble accessing their account numbers or making any change to their service. This was caused by problems performing an upgrade of its CRM software.[18]

Companies fail to define measures of success or management teams fail to review them often enough. Typically, CRM does not become ingrained in the management process of the company. And as long as it remains just another initiative, project, or computer system, it is always likely to fail, taking millions of investment dollars with it.

CRM failures are abundant as are the lessons to be learned. There are many points of failure, but strategic approaches and good planning can significantly increase the chances of success. In the following chapters, we will show how CRM can be approached and implemented in ways that mitigate its inherent risks and maximize its powerful benefits.

Key Points

- There have been many CRM failures, and reviewing the reasons for them can help mitigate risks with any CRM initiative

- The costs of failure are significant, affecting company earnings, customer satisfaction, market share, investor sentiment, internal morale, and brand perception

- Reasons for failure can be categorized into the following:

  - Poor objective setting

  - Lack of senior leadership

  - Inadequate planning and scope setting

- Implementation missteps

- Lack of change management

- Inadequate post-implementation operation

Notes

1. Lindsey Sodano, Heather Keltz, and Rod Johnson, *The Customer Management Applications Report, 2002–2007*. Boston: AMR Research, June 26, 2003.

2. Sodano, Keltz and Johnson, *The Customer Management Applications Report, 2002–2007*.

3. Meredith Levinson, "Pain Free CRM," *CIO Magazine*, May 15, 2003.

4. Laura Preslan, *Aligning Customer Investments With ROI, Metrics, and Enterprise Performance Management*. Boston: AMR Research, August 12, 2003.

5. Laura Preslan and Heather Keltz, *The Customer Management Applications Spending Report, 2003–2004*. Boston: AMR Research, August 26, 2003.

6. Alison Bass, "CIGNA's Self-Inflicted Wounds," *CIO Magazine*, March 15, 2003.

7. National Confectioners Association, "Confectionary Seasonal Sales," *www.candyusa.org/Stats/seasonal.shtml*, available as of January 22, 2004.

8. Emily Nelson and Evan Ramstad, "Trick or Treat: Hershey's Biggest Dud Has Turned Out to Be Its New Technology—At the Worst Possible Time, It Can't Fill Its Orders, Even as Inventory Grows—Kisses in the Air for Kmart," *The Wall Street Journal*, October 19, 1999; and Shelly Branch, "Hershey Will Miss Its Lowered Target for 4th Quarter," *The Wall Street Journal*, December 29, 1999.

9. Marc L. Songini, "Lexmark abandons CRM project," *COMPUTER-WORLD*, October 11, 2002, *www.computerworld.com/softwaretopics/crm/story/0,10801,75086,00.html*, available as of January 28, 2004.

10. Agilent Technologies, *Agilent Technologies reports third quarter results below expectations; drive to profitability continues*, Company press release, August 19, 2002, *www.agilent.com/about/newsroom/presrel/2002/19aug2002a.html*, available as of January 28, 2004.

11. "CarsDirect Sues Software Maker," *Los Angeles Business Journal*, December 4, 2000, *www.findarticles.com/cf_dls/m5072/49_22/67721084/p1/article.jhtml*, available as of January 28, 2004.

12. Dale Buss, "CRM horror stories: GMACCM spills the beans over failed CRM," *Context*, November 26, 2002, *http://searchcrm.techtarget.com/originalContent/0,289142,sid11_gci865340,00.html*, available as of January 28, 2004.

13. Dale Buss, "CRM horror stories: Obstacles plague Owens Corning, Perseus Development," *Context*, November 26, 2002, *http://searchcrm.techtarget.com/originalContent/0,289142,sid11_gci865343,00.html*, available as of January 28, 2004.

14. Kimberly Hill, "CPR for CRM," *CRM Daily*, March 26, 2002, *http://crm-daily.newsfactor.com/perl/story/16941.html*, available as of January 28, 2004.

15. John McCormick, "A Cheat Sheet for CRM Success," *Baseline Magazine*, March 18, 2002, *www.baselinemag.com/article2/0,3959,818844,00.asp*, available as of January 28, 2004.

16. Buss, "CRM horror stories: GMACCM spills the beans over failed CRM."

17. Jennifer Hubley, "Mutual of Omaha employees buy into customer focus," *SearchCRM*, October 30, 2001, *http://searchcrm.techtarget.com/originalContent/0,289142,sid11_gci778611,00.html*, available as of January 28, 2004.

18. Grant Gross, "CRM glitch still plagues AT&T Wireless Service," *ComputerWeekly*, 27 November 2003, *www.computerweekly.com/Article126862.htm*, available as of January 28, 2004.

CHAPTER
3

Strategy First: Aligning CRM with Company Strategy

As introduced in Chapter 1, CRM efforts that are not properly aligned with company strategy will likely produce efficiency and other gains in operational effectiveness but rarely improve competitive advantage. In many of these cases, the gains will not justify the investments made to achieve them. It is important to keep in mind that lasting gains in revenue, market share, and customer satisfaction can come only through strengthening the organization's advantages in the marketplace. CRM initiatives that fortify or enhance sources of competitive advantage have the best chance for significant and lasting returns.

Unfortunately, most initiatives designed to improve customer operations are either unaligned or improperly aligned to company strategy. This often happens because the strategy is unclear or simply not widely understood within the company. Although this book is not specifically about creating or communicating business strategies, we will show that successful CRM depends on clear and well-understood company strategy. To help demonstrate a successful approach for linking CRM to strategy, we use Harvard Professor Michael Porter's widely accepted strategy frameworks[1] to illustrate the three critical factors you can use to properly align CRM with your company's strategy:

1. Distinguish competitive advantage from pure efficiencies and other forms of operational effectiveness.

2. Identify the firm's competitive advantages.

3. Define initiatives that build or enhance the firm's sources of competitive advantage.

Leveraging Porter's well-established framework, we show how organizations can bring rigor to identifying and evaluating investments in improving customer operations.

Using an Analytical Framework for Defining Strategy

In most companies, few people outside the executive inner circle can articulate the firm's propositions to the marketplace. To make matters worse, some companies don't have a clear strategy or successive rounds of merger activity have muddied it. Recent thinking on strategy has aggravated this trend by encouraging companies to think first in terms of speed, agility, and efficiency. Yet, without a clear strategic focus that is well understood and practiced throughout the firm, all major improvement initiatives—including CRM—are unlikely to produce long-term results.

By contrast, the lasting performers carve out a focused and unique position within their industry. While, in most cases, they are very efficient companies, their true sources of advantage are more subtle. These innovative companies have not simply tried to outrun rivals, but have chosen to redefine the race or to run a different race altogether. For example, to achieve price leadership, Southwest

Airlines runs in the smaller-metro, shorter route, low-budget traveler race. It doesn't try to serve every big market and cover every route. As a result, it delivers annual profitability far above airline industry norms. At first, Southwest saw the race so differently than rival airlines that they considered their main competitors to be rail and bus services!

In order to establish a common language for the discussion around identifying strategic advantages, a brief recap of Michael Porter's analytical approach to strategy is required. In his frameworks, a company can consistently outperform rivals only if it establishes and maintains a unique strategic position. This value proposition must be coupled to a competitive scope that refers to the target set of customers. At the broadest level, there are two types of proposition: delivering the same value as competitors at lower costs (cost proposition) or providing some unique mix of value (differentiation proposition). Superior profitability follows as lower costs translate to higher margins for cost leaders, and greater value allows companies with differentiation propositions to charge higher prices.[2] Exhibit 3.1 shows the four generic strategies based on competitive scope and type of value proposition (cost or differentiation).

Wal-Mart and Southwest are good examples of companies following low cost strategy (each with a different competitive scope). Walgreen's *differentiates* with a broad competitive scope by providing high levels of convenience to its customers through handy locations and fast prescription pick-up, drive-through, and online options. Highly successful mortgage lender Option One (a division of H&R Block) targets only subprime customers with its differentiated system of service and brokerage. Discipline and time is needed to build these

Exhibit 3.1
Target Market and Value Proposition

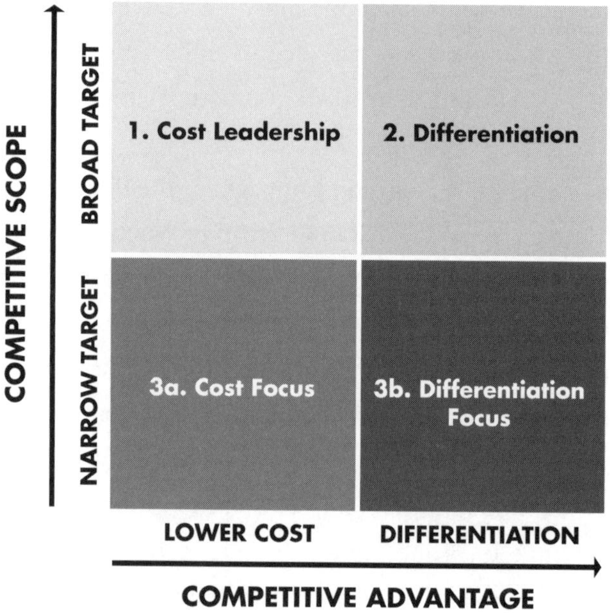

	LOWER COST	**DIFFERENTIATION**
BROAD TARGET	1. Cost Leadership	2. Differentiation
NARROW TARGET	3a. Cost Focus	3b. Differentiation Focus

COMPETITIVE SCOPE

COMPETITIVE ADVANTAGE

sustainable marketplace positions. Companies failing to pick and stick to a focus cannot create a strategic identity and meaningful position in the minds of customers.

Many CRM shortfalls are predestined by failure to link CRM goals to the firm's strategy. Without a well-established and well-articulated competitive strategy, CRM can produce only gains in efficiencies and other operational improvements. These types of improvements are necessary to avoid disadvantage in the marketplace, but do not translate to enduring advantages.

Distinguishing Competitive Advantage from Other Types of Benefits

In embarking upon CRM initiatives, many firms have confused the goal of improving the general effectiveness of operations with gaining competitive advantage. They did not clearly distinguish up-front which investments were being made to maintain acceptable Best Practices, versus those made in areas of the business that further strengthen the firm's unique position. As a result, most investments have resulted in operational improvements that, while sometimes important, are unlikely to produce significant top- or bottom-line gains. Expending too much effort on these types of changes prevents the firm from pursuing improvements that will have a greater impact on competitive advantage.

Without properly understanding and considering competitive advantage, decisions to improve operations are purely based on what Michael Porter calls *operational effectiveness* (OE). This is an umbrella term describing the attainment and extension of operational Best Practices and standards that are needed to operate within an industry. OE includes employing the most up-to-date equipment, inputs, information technology, and management techniques to improve products and processes. OE includes, but is not limited to, efficiency improvement. It also includes time-to-market, speed, reliability, and certain expected levels of service. For example, to provide full service to a broad customer set, airlines such as United and American believe OE includes state-of-the-art frequent-flier programs and on-board entertainment. These airlines believe that these services are necessary in order to meet basic customer expectations for a full-service airline.

In other words, in this area of the business, they believe this is where the OE bar has been set, and that they need this minimum level of service in order to avoid a significant *disadvantage* in the marketplace.

However, OE does not create lasting competitive advantage since competitors usually quickly match these types of improvements. Business improvements (such as CRM) result in competitive advantage only when they lower costs for cost leaders, or strengthen or further distinguish unique activities for differentiators. Indeed, within Porter's frameworks, successful strategy is judged by its ability to produce and sustain a long-term return on investment that is superior to rivals, which means producing and sustaining higher profitability.

Exhibit 3.2
Superior Long-Term Return on Investment

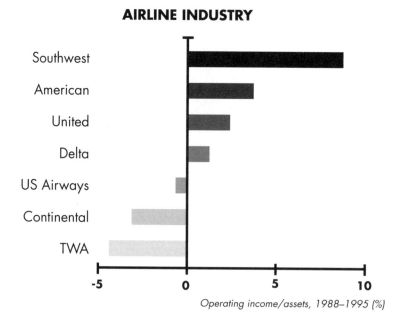

AIRLINE INDUSTRY

Operating income/assets, 1988–1995 (%)

Exhibit 3.2 shows the superior long-term return on investment (ROI) performance of Southwest Airlines, one company example referenced in this book. For CRM to be used as a competitive tool, it must be aimed at helping to improve long-term ROI. This is achieved only through strengthening competitive advantages so that lasting profitability improvements are made.

Of course, some level of continuous OE improvement is necessary to ensure the company is attaining acceptable levels of performance in each area of the business, but the lion's share of investments should go toward those areas that fortify company strategy. Exhibit 3.3 depicts the difference between OE and strategic positioning.

Exhibit 3.3
Operational Effectiveness versus Strategic Positioning

OPERATIONAL EFFECTIVENESS	STRATEGIC POSITIONING
Assimilating, attaining, and extending **BEST PRACTICES**. Updating management techniques, technology, equipment, etc.	Creating a **UNIQUE** and **SUSTAINABLE** competitive **POSITION** in the marketplace
Offering essentially the **SAME PRODUCTS/ SERVICES** as competitors, only **BETTER**	Focusing on a **DISTINCT** combination of **ACTIVITIES** that enhance strategic position and ultimately create competitive position
RUN THE SAME RACE FASTER	**CHOOSE TO RUN A DIFFERENT RACE**

This point is critical for CRM: Many CRM investments will improve OE, but priority should be given to those that produce competitive advantage. Expensive efforts that result only in OE improvements are unlikely to produce a return on the investment. Furthermore, at the same time there is an opportunity cost of not pursuing those elements of CRM that can fortify a firm's competitive strengths.

If pursued blindly, OE leads to competitive convergence, where companies get sucked into a never-ending game of catch-up. The negative experience of most Japanese companies over the past few decades typifies the dangers of competitive convergence. In the 1980s, it became obvious that Japanese companies were so good at producing identical goods more efficiently that it became extremely difficult for U.S. companies to compete. The Japanese opened an OE gap as innovations like *Total Quality Management* (TQM) and *Just-In-Time* (JIT) inventory management accelerated the speed and lowered the cost at which high-quality goods could be produced. U.S. firms swung into action to close the gap: Companies like Ford Motor, Harley Davidson, HP, and others embraced Japanese quality initiatives. As U.S. companies began to regain lost market share, many Japanese companies—especially those that lacked a long-term competitive strategy—began to struggle as their efficiency advantages eroded.

A few Japanese firms like Sony performed better because they had continuously operated efficiently *and* maintained strategic focus. Even as they became more efficient, the Japanese companies, and the many U.S. companies that emulated them, failed to create a distinctive position in the marketplace. Widespread efficiency improvements were ultimately passed through as lower prices to customers, who could not tell one company's goods from another.

In general, in Japan and the United States, the eventual winners were companies that carved out and continually fortified a strategic focus, while maintaining acceptable levels of OE.[3]

CRM should be used to help maintain acceptable levels of OE on the customer side of the business. After all, a poorly operated customer service call center or poorly kept customer records would lead to a distinct disadvantage for most companies. But in most cases these improvements will be very similar to those pursued by rivals, and so it is equally important that CRM is used to strengthen competitive advantage for the organization in the marketplace. In summary, CRM can be used to provide both OE and competitive advantage. In defining CRM investments, it is important to be able to distinguish between them.

How Competitive Advantage Manifests Itself in Operations

Having established the importance of competitive advantage to the firm and to CRM initiatives, it is important to clarify how competitive advantage is produced within the firm. In terms of daily operations, what distinguishes firms with competitive advantage from those without it? Michael Porter's research tells us that companies with competitive advantage tend to have distinct value chains. Ultimately, price and cost differences between companies derive from the many policies, processes, and activities that go into designing, producing, and delivering the firm's products or services. Cost is generated by these activities and lower-cost strategies are achieved by executing them more efficiently. To create greater value, *differentiators* must perform different activities or conduct them in different ways.

The value chain differences are not manifested in one or two activities but are built up across a large number of functions throughout the firm. Competitive advantage comes from the sum of these differences,[4] and successful companies proliferate them throughout their organizations.

So successful companies are actually collections of activities within which competitive advantage resides. Competitive advantage is the *sum of the differences*—compared to rivals—in the way things are done at the nuts-and-bolts level of the business. If the competitive advantage is not reflected within the activities of the firm, the strategy will not be executed properly. If the differences are not widespread or pronounced enough, competitive advantage will not be sustained.

Let's look more closely at Southwest Airlines. As noted, they are the low-fare airline, targeting customers who typically take short trips and seek bargain fares. Southwest has meticulously developed a unique model that provides a much lower cost-per-passenger mile than any rival. It flies mostly to less-congested secondary airports. By flying only one type of plane, Southwest reduces its training and maintenance costs. The smaller airports and planes help Southwest produce faster gate turns that increase aircraft utilization and on-time performance. Its lean gate crews turn planes around faster and, in return for higher pay, award Southwest with more flexible union contracts. It doesn't fly internationally, interchange baggage with other airlines, or offer in-flight meals. It has only one class of service.

The simple, down-to-earth, no-frills approach of Southwest Airlines is designed to support its low-fare value proposition. If customers want additional services, they can pay more to fly on other airlines. What Southwest lacks in amenities it tries to make up somewhat in style. For example, the airline screens new hires to ensure that friendly personal service dominates the company culture. Southwest consistently ranks at the top of its industry in customer satisfaction: In the first quarter of 2003, the American Consumer Satisfaction Index gave Southwest a 75 out of 100 versus the industry average of 67.[5] Flying Southwest is fun and customers love it!

Southwest's unique business model can be depicted as a highly interconnected system of activities, processes, policies, and behaviors. Exhibit 3.4 shows what Michael Porter calls the *activity system*. The larger circles represent the activities that are central to Southwest's

Exhibit 3.4
Southwest Airlines Activity System

uniqueness. The diagram is useful in showing how these activities relate to each other and how all activities take their cue from these unique approaches.

It is vital to think about sources of competitive advantage in terms of the enterprise-wide system of activities, processes, polices, and behaviors. By understanding the full picture, any strategic initiative—including CRM—can be better targeted to enhance the firm's advantages.

Identify CRM Initiatives That Fortify Competitive Advantage

As we have seen, CRM can be used both to improve operational effectiveness and enhance competitive advantage. The first step in determining which CRM initiatives to invest in is to determine which type of goal is to be pursued. We have seen that OE improvements are quickly matched by competitors. In contrast, creating enduring advantages in the marketplace leads to permanent gains in market share, price premiums, or cost advantages.[6]

There are typically two key types of goals in planning a CRM initiative:

1. Improve long-term ROI by strengthening the firm's competitive advantages, and

2. Maintain acceptable levels of operational effectiveness in all key processes and activities.

For significant and lasting top- and bottom-line gains, CRM efforts should focus chiefly on improving long-term ROI.

A critical element to consider while planning any CRM initiative is that strategies are typically formulated at the business-unit rather than the global level within the firm. This means each unit likely competes in a different industry, with a different competitive proposition and scope. Each has its own uniquely tailored value chain. There are many shared services provided by the umbrella corporation, but it is unlikely that these are sources of competitive advantage to the units.

Corporate guidelines and leadership are required in the execution of enterprise CRM projects, but one size almost certainly does not fit all when it comes to the business units. Failure to define CRM agendas tailored for each business unit is a major reason for failure of these initiatives

We have seen how the *activity system* is a useful tool for understanding the interconnected web of policies, processes, and activities that constitute a firm's competitive advantage. By mapping your unique activities—and how the entire system of activities produces competitive advantage—CRM initiatives can be formulated that strengthen your firm's unique activity system.

For example, the highly successful subprime mortgage lender found that activity-system mapping clarified the importance of the company's service culture and broker network. Many unique policies and processes within both areas contribute to the firm's competitive strengths in the marketplace. CRM improvements were designed to enhance these areas of competitive strength and purposely did not include many traditional areas—such as sales force automation—where many companies traditionally invest.

The mortgage lender's focus ensured that the best customers received unique and preferred treatments throughout each department of the firm. To do this, brokers used a customer-profitability measurement system that contained built-in customer-performance visibility. This type of focused attention to individual customers and customer segments is a characteristic found among the leading companies. They understand their advantages and create processes that enhance the benefits of their unique situations.

The CRM ideas that fortify strategy are typically different for each firm. However, our experience shows that they typically fall within five broadly defined categories:

1. Improve customer selection

2. Deliver enhanced value to customers

3. Coordinate customer interactions

4. Tailor customer-specific interactions

5. Capture feedback

Improve Customer Selection

Successful CRM requires the implementation of processes for segmenting customers and measuring performance of these segments. The capture of data from customer interactions allows the firm to build a profile of lucrative customer types. How these types of customer segments were attracted and retained provides guidance to the sales and marketing functions in attracting additional customers with similar attributes. Improved customer selection fortifies competitive advantages by fine-tuning the firm's prospecting processes and helps ensure that resources and efforts are targeted to the most appropriate prospects for the firm's value proposition. Achieving this requires several steps:

1. Defining customer segments, customer metrics, and a performance measurement process

2. Comprehensive capture of customer-interaction data. This includes information such as method of sourcing, preferred methods of buying, frequency of purchases, revenue and profit profile over time, frequency of interaction with each sales and service channel, and so on

3. Creation of target-prospect profiles and joint planning between sales and marketing for attracting, retaining, and growing target prospects

4. Regular management review of segment performance

A typical obstacle to success in implementing CRM is the failure of sales, marketing, and IT functions to work together to create and develop opportunities. When properly initiated, sales and marketing identify the specific data that are required for the analysis of customer patterns. IT then captures and organizes it for review. Through cooperation, the firm's sales, marketing, and IT departments can increase effectiveness by selecting the right kinds of customers to suit the firm's value proposition. Achieving interdepartmental teamwork is a major organizational hurdle that each firm must overcome in order to realize the full benefits of CRM.

Deliver Enhanced Value to Customers

As we have seen, CRM provides benefits to organizations by help-ing to organize and coordinate customer interactions. However, it is important to realize that CRM can also deliver direct benefits to the customer. For example, it can facilitate delivery of more accurate and helpful information during the buying process, or enable the ability of customers to buy product or receive customer support online. Rather than simply reaping internal rewards—CRM should be tar-geted on improving value delivered and the experiences created for customers.

In planning CRM investments, opportunities exist to enhance value for customers in ways that strengthen the firm's advantages. For example, many cost leaders would find their strategy enhanced through online customer self-service programs. Similarly, a leading mortgage lender—which is currently differentiated by speed of service—might introduce one-hour approvals by linking brokers and web-based loan channels with automatic underwriting systems. At the basic level, CRM can enhance competitive advantage by improving customer operations in ways that strengthen advantages.

Coordinate Customer Interactions

CRM allows firms to better manage and coordinate customer inter-actions across multiple departments. Applications can keep tabs on interactions such as orders, service requests, and product inquiries as they flow through the business. By better understanding the status of each interaction, wherever it may occur in the firm, an organization has up-to-the-minute and accurate status. It can also measure the responsiveness, cycle time, and other service-level metrics.

This coordinated approach improves operational effectiveness and can also boost competitive advantage by providing better integration between customer interaction activities. One of the hallmarks of firms with tailored value chains and competitive advantage is the high degree of "fit" between activities in the value chain. In a broad sense, fit comes in three forms:[7]

1. Consistency between activities

2. Reinforcement of activities

3. Optimization of activities

Consistency between Activities

Ensure that each department and each activity is configured and executed with the same overall goal in mind. This is no small achievement in the highly balkanized environment of modern corporations. Only the most focused of firms have achieved even this simplest level of fit. For example, mutual fund provider Vanguard aligns all its activities to its low cost strategy.[8] It minimizes portfolio turnover and does not need highly compensated money managers. Vanguard has a direct distribution approach, eschewing the use of brokers and their associated commissions. Through tailored compensation plans, it also encourages employees to continually achieve cost savings throughout the business. Consistency across the value chain ensures that the competitive advantage of activities do not cancel themselves out. It makes communicating the value proposition to employees and customers easier, and the focused approach increases the chances of good execution. CRM provides important tools for achieving consistency by allowing for standardized information capture, presentation, and workflow management across activities. It ensures that employees have control and visibility as work flows from one activity to another.

Reinforcement of Activities

In companies with pronounced strategic advantages, activities are designed and performed in ways that improve the effectiveness of other activities. For example, going beyond simple consistency, Neutrogena's marketing activities are self-reinforcing.[9] The company invests in relationships with dermatologists to gain endorsements from the medical community. At the same time, they distribute product through upscale hotels, which are keen to co-brand a soap recommended by doctors. These marketing and distribution activities feed off each other to reinforce Neutrogena's mild, medicinal cleansing brand attributes.

Implemented properly, CRM creates reinforcement for the key activities across the value chain. For example, Walgreen's stores and online pharmacy are designed to bolster customer convenience. By implementing a national customer database, automatically available to any store, customers can order online and pick up anywhere in the country—even changing plans at the last minute. Only CRM's central data platform and applications, when configured to automate and integrate disparate sales channels, can provide this functionality. In the Walgreen's example, CRM elevates previously separate buying channel activities into a mutually reinforcing more beneficial whole for the customer.

Optimization of Activities

Once activities are consistent and mutually reinforcing, leading firms invest in optimizing them. This could take the form of eliminating redundancy, minimizing wasted effort, improving product design through better feedback from customers, and designing product or service plans so that customers can perform certain service activities themselves. Leading casino operator Harrah's bases its strategic positioning on attracting retirees (low-rollers) interested mainly in playing slots. Harrah's developed various programs and benefits designed to attract these customers and keep them loyal. One of these involved developing at each property a "frequent player" tracking card that accumulated benefits with increasing play. After the initial introduction of the card, Harrah's felt it could significantly enhance this idea by allowing customers to use their cards at all Harrah's properties. The first step was to implement a national database called the Winner's Information Network.[10]

Analytical tools and models were implemented to help spot patterns in the data. The models and technology were also patented to protect the innovations. Next steps included training local properties in using the tools and models.

David Norton, Vice President of Loyalty Marketing at Harrah's, said the program has contributed over $100 million of additional revenues since its inception. He also noted that over 70 percent of Harrah's revenue is now tracked—meaning that it can be traced to an individual cardholder. There are currently six million active cardholders.[11]

The upshot is that Harrah's introduced an innovative way to drive business with its customers and they continue to enhance and optimize those activities and processes. The more nuanced the programs become, the harder it is for competitors to emulate them.[12]

These sorts of efforts to optimize existing advantages are the keystone of successful CRM. Too often, CRM implementation takes on a Hail Mary flavor when, in fact, simple creative ideas that build on existing processes are likely to produce bigger long-term gains. To identify ideas for tailoring and optimizing, Harrah's used a sophisticated system for gathering and analyzing customer insight. We will see in the next chapter how these types of approaches work and how they can be used to drive long-term returns for your company.

Competitive advantage resides in the tightly nested system of activities with the firm. Activities are designed, integrated, and implemented to pursue the firm's strategic themes. The system as a whole is more important than any individual activity. The sustainability of competitive advantage is based on how difficult (or undesirable) it is for competitors to emulate a rival's value chain. As shown in previous examples, the wider, more unique, and deeply nested the web of activities is, the harder it is for rivals to emulate. This is why it is critical for firms to continue investing in strengthening its sources of competitive advantages through initiatives such as CRM.

When embarking upon CRM, it is critical to keep in mind the firm's need to continually strengthen strategy. Unless the goal is to achieve simple gains in operational effectiveness, CRM must serve to strengthen and optimize the firm's activity system. It must be implemented in a tailored way, behind a strategic theme that helps further distinguish the firm's operations. Most CRM initiatives to date have failed to approach the opportunity for CRM success in this manner.

Tailor Customer-Specific Interactions

Once customers have been segmented and their value and needs identified, the firm can begin serving segments (and even individual customers) in unique ways. This requires implementing unique

74

policies, processes, and activities based on the needs and values of different customers. By tailoring how customers are treated, the firm can control the service level and costs associated with each type of customer. This also allows the firm to build loyalty and gather more insights into the needs of these customers. For example, the mortgage lender described earlier might implement an expedited loan application and different underwriting rules for its best customers. Customer-level tailoring can add another layer of uniqueness to the firm's distinctive value chain.

With CRM, comprehensive customer-level tailoring is now possible. CRM provides tools for segmenting customers, measuring value, capturing insight, and configuring and automating the various tailored service levels associated with each customer. It also helps to coordinate and integrate differentiated service levels across the enterprise.

Capture Feedback

One of the key benefits of CRM is the ability to capture essential information from marketing, sales, and service activities. As customers interact with the firm through person-to-person and electronic channels, information can be captured, centralized, and organized for review. After implementing CRM, it is difficult in most organizations to prioritize action based on the great quantity of information now available. For firms with clear understanding of their distinct advantages, customer feedback can be prioritized and used to continue improving the firm's capabilities and approaches in the areas that most impact its competitive advantage. Customer feedback is a major input in the continuing efforts to tailor the firm's value chain, as well as to deliver value to individual or segments of customers.

Key Points

- CRM failures are often due to the lack of a clear and focused company strategy. CRM should not be attempted if this type of strategy is not in place.

- CRM can help make customer-related operations more effective, but this is not the same as creating competitive advantage. Gains in competitive advantage are measured by sustained gains in profitability over rivals.

- CRM creates competitive advantage when it strengthens the web of policies, processes, and activities that represent the unique way the company does business, either by making it more efficient or emphasizing unique approaches and methods that lead to greater value.

Notes

1. Michael E. Porter, "What Is Strategy?" *Harvard Business Review*. Boston: Harvard Business School Press, November 1, 1996.

2. Ibid.

3. Ibid.

4. Ibid.

5. American Customer Satisfaction Index, May 21, 2003, *www.theacsi.org/first_quarter.htm#air*, available as of February 3, 2004.

6. Porter, "What Is Strategy?"

7. Ibid.

8. Ibid.

9. Ibid.

10. Gary Loveman, "Diamonds in the Data Mine," *Harvard Business Review*, #R0305H. Boston: Harvard Business School Press, May 1, 2003; and Martha Rogers, "Harrah's Takes the Gamble Out of Customer Loyalty," *SearchCRM*, June 11, 2002, *http://searchcrm. techtarget.com/originalContent/0,289142,sid11_gci832166,00.htm*, available as of February 3, 2004.

11. Rogers, "Harrah's Takes the Gamble Out of Customer Loyalty."

12. Loveman, "Diamonds in the Data Mine."

Customer Intelligence: The Science of Customer Insight

The history of business is replete with examples of how long-held beliefs were overturned by innovations, creative thinking, and new approaches. Market leaders have often been toppled by upstarts touting innovative business models that anticipate new or undiscovered customer needs. For example, within the computer industry, IBM missed the mini-computer trend, ceding the market to DEC, which subsequently turned the keys to the vault over to PC makers. Both companies failed to detect nascent and fast-emerging demand for personalized and more flexible computer power within the various departments of their customers. In a bold move, Microsoft created a business model based on software, flying in the face of IBM and DEC's hardware-dominated, software-giveaway strategies. This seemingly upside-down business model anticipated personal computer use and allowed Microsoft to become the most valuable company in the world. In the retail industry, Wal-Mart's discount format toppled Sears from industry leadership, and retailers of fashionable young women's clothing are being rocked by top European retailer Zara's innovative model. Zara is fundamentally changing the fashion retail industry by designing, producing, and stocking its shelves with new fashionable items in six weeks rather than the traditional six months. Similarly, casino operator Harrah's has demonstrated that low-rollers can be more profitable customers than high-rollers in the gaming industry. These companies overturn conventional wisdom, and, in doing so, often change their industries forever. The success of Harrah's and Zara demonstrates that industry beliefs long held as self-evident were actually outmoded ideas in need of modernization or simply false.

Executive blind spots are not limited to upstart new entrants; in fact, major structural trends within industries are often missed or underestimated. For example, few companies in the electronics, manufacturing, and high-tech industries foresaw that complex technical goods would eventually be manufactured in third-world countries. Yet this trend became pervasive against the fervent beliefs of experienced industry executives.

Conducting business as usual seems to be a common trait in the human condition. Recent upheaval in the baseball world provides an interesting parallel. Baseball officials and executives have been collecting and acting on the same kinds of player and team-performance statistics for decades. Yet empirical evidence overwhelmingly points to less obvious statistics, such as on-base and slugging percentage, as being more indicative of player contribution and team success than, say, batting average. This is an amazing revelation—after all, millions of people have been gazing at baseball statistics and scoring games for decades without noticing a problem. Over the past five years, the Oakland A's have run their team according to a new wisdom—and during this period have won the second most number of games in baseball with the second lowest payroll. In the recent book, *Moneyball*,[1] Michael Lewis describes how Oakland takes a dramatically different approach to running its team. It has invested in computer systems, databases, and Ivy League statistics experts. When drafting, trading, promoting, and fielding players, it makes decisions based on players' statistical performances and the proven importance of various statistics to the number of team wins. This is in contrast to tradition, where teams made decisions based on statistics less strongly correlated to wins, plus the intuition of scouts about how a player will develop. Already, a couple of other teams have hired general managers with quantitative backgrounds and Oakland-like philosophies. Undoubtedly, the change will come slowly. In baseball, as well as in other businesses, people tend to stick doggedly to the traditions and ideas of the past.

The point of these examples is to demonstrate that deep and long-held beliefs about customers and the marketplace hold sway in most organizations. Many of these beliefs are right but a significant number are wrong. Innovations occur continuously, and many can dramatically reshape businesses as they unfold. But most companies are followers rather than trendsetters and they end up scrambling to react as they finally realize the full extent of change. Adapting to and seizing innovative opportunities means having the facts and analytical capability to anticipate change and act ahead of the competition.

Like the baseball executives at Oakland's competitors, most senior executives we talk to do not fully realize that false conventional wisdom pervades their industries and companies. For busy leaders, it is very difficult to step back and conduct rigorous research and analysis while immersed in the everyday running of the business. Companies are meant to produce and sell products and services to customers, not run science labs. But scientific and statistical thinking is exactly what they need to improve their competitive positions. Customer insight *must* become a science within organizations wishing to be successful. Many firms think they already have a pretty good process for capturing data about customers and the marketplace, but in fact they don't.

Many companies feel they do an okay job of leveraging data to gather insights, whereas in reality this rarely happens. These same companies believe that data and customer insight is shared across the organization, but it's usually not the case. There are a few scattered databases and masses of information but few systematic ways to mine, study, and leverage it.

In general, marketing and sales do not use data to create and test hypotheses in the marketplace. Instead, they rely on intuition. New ideas occur to people within organizations all the time—but rarely are they born from the data and seldom are the marketplace results of these ideas captured to enhance the data.

By relying mainly on the gut feel of marketers and salespeople, companies guarantee the perpetuation of shopworn beliefs. Some of these ideas are right and some are dead wrong. How do you know which are which? The answer is to let the facts be your guide. Gaining and using customer insight is a science not an art. The lessons of *Moneyball* should be applied to your business. Companies seeking to improve their profitability will capture and systematically analyze data, create models, generate new ideas, run marketplace experiments, measure results, and adopt the things that work. Successful companies back up their brands, sales, and marketing approaches by creating an infrastructure of data, facts, and analysis behind the scenes. They work to create processes, systems, and databases that ensure that every go-to-market idea and approach is grounded in measurable, provable business facts.

How Harrah's Used Customer Insight to Turn the Tables on the Gaming Industry

Returning to an example introduced earlier, casino company Harrah's Entertainment Inc. has had great success in targeting "low-rollers" in recent years.[2] In fact, the approach was so successful that recent revenue growth and stock appreciation had far outpaced the gaming industry. By 2002, the company posted more than $4 billion in revenue, $235 million in net income, and a streak of 16 straight quarters of "same-store" revenue growth. Harrah's now has 26 casinos in 13 states.

> The results are so impressive that other casino operators are copying some of Harrah's more discernible methods. Wall Street analysts are also beginning to see Harrah's—long a dowdy also-ran in the flashy casino business—as gaining an edge on its rivals. Harrah's stock price has risen quickly as investors have received news of the marketing results. And the company's earnings have more than doubled in the past year."[3]

Harrah's CEO explained how the company has dramatically improved customer loyalty, even during a challenging economy.[4] For Harrah's, CRM consists of two key elements. First, it uses database marketing and decision-science-based analytical tools to ensure that operational and marketing decisions are based on fact rather than intuition. Second, it uses this insight, together with marketing experiments, to develop and implement service-delivery strategies that are finely tuned to customer needs.

In 1998, Harrah's decided that it wanted to change from an operations-driven company that viewed every casino as a stand-alone property to a marketing-driven company with a holistic view of its properties and customers. In effect, it wanted to move away from an OE-driven organization to one with a clear value proposition and competitive scope. This allowed Harrah's to focus its activities throughout the enterprise and meaningfully build its brand. In 1997, it had already implemented a loyalty program called Total Gold, which was a frequent-player program based on airline industry loyalty schemes. At first, the program was not highly differentiated within the gaming industry, varied across properties, and did not motivate customers to consolidate their gaming at Harrah's properties. However, customer data derived from the program began the process of building the company's data mine. For example, Total Gold player cards recorded customer activity at various points of sale—including slot machines, restaurants, and shops. Soon, the database contained millions of transactions and valuable information about customer preferences and spending habits.

Once the data-mining process started in earnest, the first fact that jumped out was that Harrah's customers spent only 36 percent of their gaming dollars with the company. Also, they discovered that 26 percent of customers produced 82 percent of the revenues. Statistical analysis further revealed that the best customers were not the "high-rollers" so coveted by the rest of the industry. In fact, the best customers turned out to be slot-playing middle-aged folks or retired teachers, bankers, and doctors with time and discretionary income. They did not necessarily stay at a hotel, but often visited a casino just for the evening. Surveys of these customers told Harrah's that they visited casinos primarily because of the intense anticipation and excitement of gambling itself.

Given this insight, Harrah's decided to consolidate its strategy around these choice customers and focus branding, marketing, and the types of products and services being offered on meeting their needs. For example, Harrah's concentrated all of its advertising around the feeling of exuberance gambling produced for the segment. It developed quantitative models to predict lifetime value of these customers and used them to center marketing and service-delivery programs on increasing customer loyalty. It found that customers who had a very happy experience with Harrah's increased their spending on gambling at Harrah's by 24 percent a year. In contrast, unhappy experiences led to 10 percent declines. In an indication of success in capturing greater wallet-share, the programs dramatically increased the amount of cross-market (multiple property) play. This grew from 13 percent in 1997 to 23 percent in 2000.

Harrah's spent more time integrating data across properties, developing models, mining the data, and running marketing experiments. This, in turn, generated even more information on customer preferences and led to more insightful marketing and service delivery programs. Harrah's realized that the data, coupled with decision-science tools that allowed it to predict long-term value, enabled it to target marketing and service programs at individual player preferences. As Harrah's CEO said:

> The further we get ahead and the more tests we run, the more we learn. The more we understand our customers, the more substantial the switching costs that we put in place, and the farther ahead we are of our competitors' efforts. That is why we are running as fast as we can.[5]

Strategic focus, customer insight, and resulting continuous optimization of its unique approach has propelled it to the primary position within its industry.

Seven Dimensions of Customer Insight

As we saw with the Harrah's example, customer insight can come in many forms from many sources. It may relate to the age or gender of a customer and the customer's specific behavior before or after purchase. The information can be gathered electronically at the point of purchase, through face to face interactions, or emerge from analysis of a database containing customer-buying history. In this section, we provide a framework to help categorize the various types of customer information that organizations typically seek to capture. We then lay out a process through which information can be gathered, analyzed, and translated into action. We use seven broad dimensions to describe the customer information that firms typically seek to capture, and below show example elements that companies tend to seek within each dimension:

- *What and how often customers buy:*

  - The products and services each customer is buying and has bought in the past.

  - The product configurations, additional features, service plans, and other additional elements bought.

  - The frequency of purchases of each product.

  - The products or substitute products each customer buys or has bought from competitors.

Note: We have found that most organizations do not spend enough time assessing "share-of wallet" information. Usually, the first visibility they have into this is the market-share statistics gathered well after the fact.

- *How they decide what to buy:*

    - What is the customer's decision-making process?

    - What information is needed for them to make a purchase decision?

    - What interactions are needed to make a purchase decision?

    - How long is the decision-making cycle?

- *Why customers buy:*

    - What are the key decision-making criteria (e.g., price, convenience, quality, brand association, etc.)?

    - What psychological factors come into play?

- *How customers buy:*

    - What channels do they use to buy products?

    - What interactions are required to conduct the purchase?

    - Do they require special receipt, quality assurance, or delivery options?

- *What are their internal/personal circumstances:*

    - What are the customer's financial circumstances?

- What are their strategic priorities?

- How do customers put the product to use once purchased?

- Do they perform activities in preparation for purchase or receipt of goods/service?

- What other related activities or circumstances might impact buying decision/process or product use?

Note: For business-to-business transactions, it is often very useful to map out the customer's value chain in order to best learn how products and services are truly put to use. This process creates opportunities to change the point at which the firm interacts with, or adds value to, the customer. For example, some firms have changed their relationship point with the customer by taking over inventory management or replenishment using pre-agreed rules.

- *What relevant external factors are in play:*

  - What are the competitive strengths and weaknesses of customer versus rivals?

  - Are there structural trends within the customer's industry (e.g. outsourcing, commoditization, etc.)?

  - What are the key macroeconomic factors influencing the customer?

  - What regulatory conditions impact the customer?

  - Are there any other key factors affecting the customer's circumstances?

- *What post-sale interactions do customers require:*

  - What type and frequency of support does the customer require after purchase?

  - What information does the customer require after purchase?

  - Which channels does the customer prefer to interact through?

  - How often is the product returned or sent back in need of repair?

  - How often is repair or modification required due to specific customer circumstances?

It is clear that a tremendous amount of useful information can be captured about customers. Yet one of the most common mistakes made in building comprehensive data-gathering processes is assembling too much data and organizing it poorly. When this occurs, the data become difficult to analyze and accessible only by IT-skilled resources. However, when data gathering is implemented properly, it yields easily-understood information that can be put to use in ways that improve the effectiveness of both operations and strategy. Some of the concrete improvements that result from systematic collection of customer data are shown below:

- *Increased marketing effectiveness.*

  Use of customer characteristics and buying patterns to segment the customer base into groups of similar types of customers allows the firm to craft tailored marketing approaches, sales, and service plans for each group.

- *Tailored service levels.*

  Use of segment characteristics, and a detailed understanding of customer needs, to customize interactions and the types and levels of service delivered to customers.

- *Improved product development processes.*

  Customer insight is fed back to improve product design and convey implicit information such as refined designs that eliminate common service complaints or recurring defects.

- *Increased customer profitability.*

  Customer-performance metrics and cost-to-serve metrics allow firms to deploy resources and budget to better manage under-performing customers and optimize highly profitable (or high potential) customers.

- *Increased pricing effectiveness.*

  Understanding pricing, discounts, and performance against volume purchase agreements can be tremendously revealing in most organizations. Most firms find realized price is well below expectations. Pricing rules and discipline can be improved based on better insight into individual and customer segment performance.

- *More effective deployment of firm-wide resources.*

  Use of segment value, needs, and performance data as the driver of resource deployment and focus throughout the firm. Resource deployment is rigid and political within most firms, meaning that at any given time too few resources are focused on the best opportunities. When customer-performance data is part of regular management reviews, resource deployment usually improves.

Define a Scientific Process for Leveraging Customer Insight

A systematic process for gaining and leveraging customer insight, as shown in Exhibit 4.1, analyzes existing customer information, gathers new information, generates and tests hypotheses, reviews results, and adjusts marketing and operating methods accordingly. This is a process, not a project—it's a continuous approach to driving customer intelligence and more targeted marketing. Results *must* be measured. Facts that are captured guide ideas for action and only those actions that are measurably successful are continued.

The science of customer insight has three key steps at the highest level:

1. Capture and analyze customer data from operations.

2. Analyze the customer's internal circumstances.

3. Translate insight into action.

Exhibit 4.1
Customer Insight Model

CUSTOMER'S PERSPECTIVE → FEEDBACK DATA PROCESS ANALYSIS ACTION ← COMPANY VIEWPOINT

CUSTOMER INSIGHT MODEL

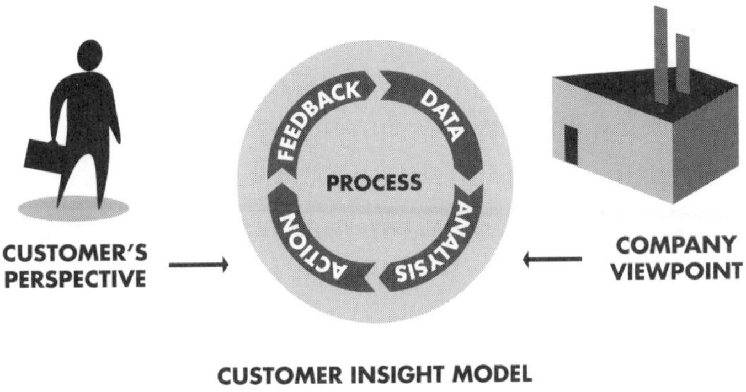

Step 1: Capture and Analyze Customer Data from Operations

Let's look at capturing and analyzing customer data from operations in more detail, by breaking the data into the following subsets:

- Review historical data.

- Create predictive value models.

- Create customer segments and associated prospecting and servicing plans.

Review Historical Data

Whether mined or not, every organization has multiple sources of customer information. Some of the information is likely to be locked up in Enterprise Resource Planning (ERP) or Supply Chain Management (SCM) systems. Other sources typically include legacy sales or marketing databases. In most organizations there will be plenty of data but it will be poorly organized. Consolidating, centralizing, and cleaning customer data is essential. Once this is achieved, the reconstituted data should be rigorously reviewed to reveal useful information. The historical data sources alone, for example, can lead to startling discoveries such as who the most profitable customers are and which service lines are most in demand. As we saw earlier in the Harrah's example, data analysis revealed the insight that a previously unidentified customer segment was far more lucrative than others, and this knowledge led to fundamental changes in the company's strategy.

Create Predictive Value Models

Understanding the value of certain individual or customer segments is the next step in gaining customer insight. Understanding their top-line impacts is relatively easy and simply requires a consolidation of revenue performance from various financial systems. Understanding the costs of serving customers and determining their *future* value is more involved. In most organizations, costs are typically associated with customers through the use of simple allocation algorithms. However, such an approach results in a misleading cost picture. The true cost of serving various customers is often a significant eye-opener. For example, in recent work for a large distribution company, we completed an activity-based analysis of customer value. Surprisingly, the results revealed that less than 2 percent of the customer population created 50 percent of the total Earnings Before Interest and Taxes (EBIT) contribution. Furthermore, a majority of the losses were generated by 1.83 percent of the customers. The allocation models previously in place produced very different results, leading to the false belief that many more of the company's customers were profitable than was actually the case. At Harrah's, high-maintenance high-rollers turned out to be expensive to serve and disloyal. Although counterintuitive, low-rollers represented the profit jackpot.

Once revenue and cost is understood, companies should—as shown in the Harrah's example—analyze the characteristics of the profitable customers. How are they alike? How often do they buy? How do they prefer to buy? How long do they remain customers? Creating a predictive model of the value of these groups of customers is the next step in the scientific enlightenment of customer management.

Create Customer Segments and Associated Prospecting and Servicing Plans

It would be tempting to use historical data and a new understanding of the characteristics of profitable customers to declare victory. But there is more to the story. Certain customers have similar characteristics, needs, and/or value to the firm. Using customer segments to organize the customer base can facilitate tailored service and prospecting plans for each segment. This framework can galvanize the various parts of the organization around specific goals for each segment. This exercise in customer segmentation is vitally important and many firms gloss over it. Most companies are shocked when they review their properly calculated customer profitability data. For example, they often find that, like the high-rollers referenced above, some customers buy in great volume but are too expensive to service. In addition, some customers are profitable but buy infrequently. Often, firms find that a different approach is required to improve profitability within many of the segments.

The "best" customers are probably also those most coveted by competitors. The key is finding a group of profitable customers that is best suited to the firm's strategy. Sometimes that means focusing on a less-profitable segment and creating new ways to serve them more profitably, as shown in the Harrah's example. Paychex, the hugely profitable payroll provider, focuses on small businesses—the customers that their competitor, ADP, could not target successfully. Paychex found cheaper ways to serve small businesses, by, for example, collecting payroll information over the phone rather than training staff at a client site to carry out the task. And Enterprise Rent-a-Car provided referral fees to auto dealers and mechanics to generate business from same-city, consumer car renters.

Broadly speaking, the key is to target a customer group that satisfies two criteria:

1. The segment is, or has the potential to be, highly profitable.

2. The firm's current or potential unique advantages with these customers allows it to create and retain an edge over competitors.

Step 2: Analyze the Customer's Internal Circumstances

It has been well documented that it is rare for a market-leading company to be the first to identify and capitalize on new directions in the marketplace.[6] It is typically not the current players that seize emerging demand opportunities and major trends. One reason for this is that most companies make too many assumptions about what their customers actually value. They think they already know what customers want. At one point, these companies did know, and they grew large and successful as a result. But with growth comes organizational complexity, breakdowns in communication, internal distractions such as politics and reorganizations, and a gradual loss of touch with customers. Consequently, most established companies are far too internally focused. Moreover, they are enamored of and tied too closely to their current products, services, and modes of delivering them.

A scientific process for analyzing data will deliver results, but it must go hand-in-hand with a much better understanding of customers and the willingness to admit shortcomings. In understanding customers, companies would do well to adopt a more empathetic approach, putting themselves in their customers' shoes, and being prepared to admit that they are far from perfect at meeting and anticipating their needs. But in keeping with the theme of this chapter, and the book as a whole, empathy and self-awareness can be helped along by using a more scientific approach. Combined with the enterprise's customer data and analysis infrastructure that we saw in Step 1 of the science of customer insight, adding empathy and self-awareness can generate powerful market knowledge. The two key subsets of Step 2 are:

- Understand your customers' competitive environment

- Analyze the buyer value chain

Understand Your Customers' Competitive Environment

Surveying customers to identify their needs can be approached in many proven ways. These include product sampling, focus groups, multidimensional scaling, conjoint analysis, and hedonic price analysis. These methods identify customers' preferences, needs, and buying patterns. Most companies survey customers using one or more of these approaches. For example, a financial services company recently conducted a detailed internal- and external-value/needs analysis. The company looked at its customer base and found four primary, needs-based groups of customers. The most interesting difference among them was the preferred style and frequency of communication.

Before the company undertook the study, it had used a standard approach through which to communicate with customers on a regular basis regarding internal products-and-solutions offerings. The company had assumed that all of its customers desired regular contact and updates on new financial services offers and opportunities. However, when the external-needs analysis was completed, it was revealed that different customer groups desired different levels of communication. For example, the analysis showed that customers living in houses built before the 1960s and with more than three bathrooms, were most likely to enjoy frequent contact with the company, while customers with more than two properties were unlikely to want frequent contact.

External surveys such as these can show only what customers know they want or need. It cannot identify needs or desires that customers cannot express or don't know they have. Needs and desires are often psychological in nature and aren't easily assessed through surveys or focus groups. For example, Harley Davidson has known for a long time that it is selling lifestyle, not transportation. Similarly, car manufacturers understand that selling a car means appealing to a buyer's affinities with, or ambitions to join, a certain demographic group. Because customers often can't articulate—or may be unwilling to admit—their motives, determining needs and desires requires going well beyond customer surveys. The key to uncovering underlying motivations—so vital to creating additional value or new products and services for customers—is to get at the core of why customers make particular choices. Begin the empathy process by getting yourself into your customers' shoes. Observing customers in their own environment provides insights that disclose new needs and opportunities.[7]

Marketing and research firms such as Carton Donofrio Partners deploy teams of cultural anthropologists to observe consumers in their natural habitat. The goal is to gain direct insights into customers' needs and preferences, and to understand how a product or service does or does not add value to them.

In one example, Carton Donofrio Partners used cultural anthro-pologists in a project for Gore.[8] They discovered a segment of the target population in the Gore-Tex line that did not buy outdoor apparel as frequently as would be expected by avid outdoorsmen. But the research also showed that when the selected subset did purchase outdoorwear, they always bought high-end, authentic merchandise. Using this customer insight, Gore introduced new, higher price/higher performance products in order to satisfy the niche mar-ket. The upshot was that the introductions of GORE-TEX PacLiteK® and GORE-TEX XCR were among the most success-ful launches Gore has ever undertaken.

Analyze the Buyer Value Chain

One of the best ways to bring some method to the customer-empa-thy process is to properly understand how customers intend to put your product or service to use. How do they take delivery, store, and maintain it? How much preparation is required to use it, and is the product or service put to use by an individual or in a group setting? How do they replenish or return defective product? Whether the customer is a business or a consumer and you are selling computers or balding treatments, there are many factors in play after the product is purchased.[9]

In other words, what is the value chain of activities that goes on after the customer buys from you? Michael Porter advises companies to map out their customers' value chains to understand how a product or service is really put to use. For business customers, a vendor's prod-uct or service, in the end, must serve to either lower costs or improve performance. Mapping a value chain for a business-to-business customer relationship is relatively straightforward and is also a useful exercise in analyzing business-to-consumer relationships.

In a business-to-business example, Dell carved out a leadership position with corporate PC customers. It spent time understanding what goes on after Dell PCs are purchased, by examining how the computers are stored, what preparation is required before distribution to employees, what software must be installed, how companies keep track of the PCs once they are put to use across the enterprise, and what is the repair process. In order to fully appreciate the activities that surround the corporate purchase, use, and ownership of a PC, Dell deployed teams to work in its corporate-customer environments. This analysis led to Dell's decision to increase its value to customers. For example, Dell invested in a high-speed network on the PC production line so that corporate customers' software installations could be completed during the manufacturing process. Dell also added asset tags to help the management of the PCs, and streamlined and customized the procurement process. Dell changed the points at which it interacts within the customer's value chain and, as a result, became a harder to replace, more strategic vendor.

To truly understand customer needs, simple surveys are not enough. Companies must appreciate the psychological buying factors and the full set of activities that surround the product or service that is being offered. More often than not, this more complete understanding will lead to many ideas that add value for customers and increase advantages over rivals.

Step 3: Translate Insight into Action

Generate Ideas for Improvements and Test Them

Customer insight generates ideas or hypotheses around new ways to create value and competitive advantage. These hypotheses should be tested through marketplace experiments and the results measured. In this approach, successful experiments are adopted and unsuccessful ones cast aside. Whatever the decision may be, further valuable insight is generated and added to the firm's growing data arsenal. Experiments might consist of a new marketing campaign or a special way of communicating with a particular group of customers. Or they involve an overhaul of the service levels associated with certain types of customers—perhaps high-potential customers deserve special treatments, or traditionally unprofitable customers must be served in different, more profitable ways.

Bank of America has developed a formal experimentation approach to test new ideas before full release to the marketplace. These ideas are tested in bank branches that are specially designated as test locations. Other branches serve as controls, so that results of experiments can be properly evaluated. The bank follows a rigorous approach to experimentation, implementing a formal process and adopting standard controls from the world of science to increase the validity and accuracy of the experiments. In this way, new ideas such as redesigned branches, greeters, or TVs in the waiting line are tested before being implemented. For example, in examining queuing times at branches, they found that customers' perceived wait times were 30 percent greater than actual wait times. To counter this mis-perception, the bank tested placement of televisions carrying CNN in checkout lines. Even after the novelty period wore off, the bank found that perceived waiting time was reduced by 15 percent versus that at control locations. Accurate results from the trial sites provide the means to properly calculate return on investment (ROI) and make better investment decisions.[10]

Continuously Optimize the Value Chain by Tailoring Processes and Activities

Customer insight and experimentation is a continuous process. In practice, it is indeed a symbiotic relationship, with marketplace results feeding back to help provide even deeper insights. Harrah's continues to invest and reinvest in the science of customer insight. Healthcare insurance provider Wellpoint Health Networks creates and maintains sophisticated pricing models by continually building a vast database on the costs of specific medical procedures. Progressive Insurance focuses on high-risk drivers. This is a seemingly dubious strategy until you understand how they do it.

The company models driver types in increasing detail, collecting information on the factors affecting risk. Progressive was one of the first insurance companies to analyze crash data. They studied information provided by the Highway Loss Data Institute and found great variations in the cost of repairing different vehicle models and how well these cars protected passengers from injury. This led to special pricing based on vehicle types. Competitors soon followed suit and such practices are now standard. But Progressive continues to tailor and optimize its sophisticated data collection and analysis processes, and the results show that they consistently outperform competitors.[11]

Tailoring operations based on insight can lead to the use of differential treatments for increasingly finer segments of the customer base. Adaptation based on information leads to higher levels of optimization and makes it harder for rivals to match a firm's marketplace edge.

A scientific customer-insight process drives the way firms target, attract, serve, and retain customers. Exhibit 4.2 shows how insight begins to drive how value is delivered, what capabilities are required, and how the capabilities are deployed. Given the importance of these potential advantages, it is clear that most firms must invest more in their customer-insight processes.

Building Blocks Required to Implement a Customer Insight Infrastructure

We have described the scientific process for generating customer insight, testing new ideas, and remodeling operations accordingly. However, most organizations don't have a clear view of the business and technology components required. In this section, we describe these key elements, showing how companies should get started and then gradually build advanced processes and techniques for generating and responding to customer insight.

Exhibit 4.3 summarizes the customer intelligence building blocks, mapping the four key stages required to achieve an advanced customer-insight operation.

Stage 1: Customer Intelligence Infrastructure

In the mid- to late-1990s, organizations started creating enterprise and divisional data warehouses that provided easy access to information.

Exhibit 4.2
Delivering the Customer Value Propositions

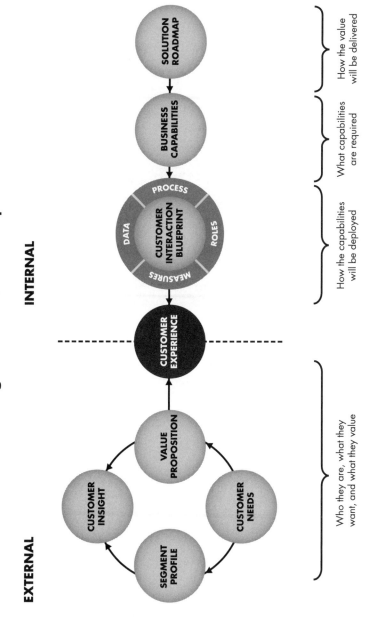

Exhibit 4.3
Customer Intelligence Roadmap

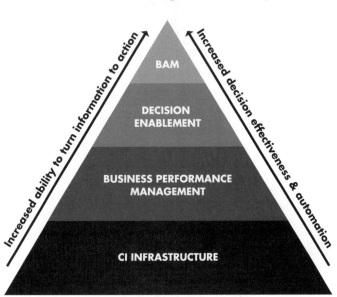

The core infrastructures supporting these initiatives were data cleansing and transformation tools, reporting architecture, batch architecture, and database architecture. At the time, the focus was on more timely access to information in order to make more informed decisions.

The goal behind these implementations was the development of an enterprise-wide information infrastructure to support operational decisions. The first step usually entailed accumulating vast amounts of information from all corners of the company to provide a comprehensive view of the customer. The next step leverages query and reporting tools to allow business analysts to slice and dice the information as easily as possible. As mentioned earlier in this chapter, there are many sources of customer-related data. This data typically resides within call centers, sales, distributors, marketing, Enterprise Resource Planning (ERP), and supply chain databases.

After deciding which records represent the accurate dataset, an infrastructure of data warehouses and data-marts is implemented. This allows various departments access to databases designed specifically to suit their needs. For example, marketers may seek data that analyzes sales resulting from special promotions, so that they may track profitability of customer segments within designated distribution channels. Similarly, telesales managers may want to track cross-selling success from one product to another, or for particular customer segments. When properly organized, the customer insight (CI) infrastructure allows for the creation of comprehensive analysis and reporting on customer-related issues.

By creating an enterprise solution, architecture, and philosophy through an enterprise data warehouse, a company can leverage customer information across the firm and graduate to more sophisticated customer-insight techniques. During the CI infrastructure development stage, companies will typically address the following:

- A more complete and accurate single view of the customer, including demographics, behavior/purchase history, promotion, and contact history.

- A set of standard reports that can be run across the business for any time interval.

- Self-service reporting tools that empower business analysts to produce ad hoc reports and analysis.

- The ability to create data-marts for specific point functions (such as retention reporting, sales velocity, etc.) in a matter of weeks.

- The ability to speed up data research projects such as those focused on customer segmentation, customer value analysis, and customer issue root analysis.

The customer-intelligence (CI) building blocks are the basic tools that facilitate access to data residing across the company's various databases. The schema in Exhibit 4.4 describes the components of the CI layer.

Stage 2: Business Performance Management

Once the foundation is in place, companies can more easily implement formal processes for tracking key performance metrics. We refer to this as *Business Performance Management*. Many organizations that have invested in their CI infrastructures have realized that although data warehouses solve many problems, they can also cause others. In general, plentiful, accurate data provides tremendous benefits to the organization. But sophisticated tools and reams of information can confuse end users who may not be able to articulate their information needs in ways that the data-infrastructure program understands. Or they can become overwhelmed by the volume of data available. Sometimes users are simply busy executing and the right questions to ask may not occur to them or ideas may not come up in time to correct an emerging problem or take advantage of a business trend.

These types of issues usually result from information overload or the inability to easily interpret large quantities of information. In addition to a surfeit of information, executives often cannot find answers to relatively simple questions. For this reason, many organizations are

Exhibit 4.4
CI Infrastructure Components

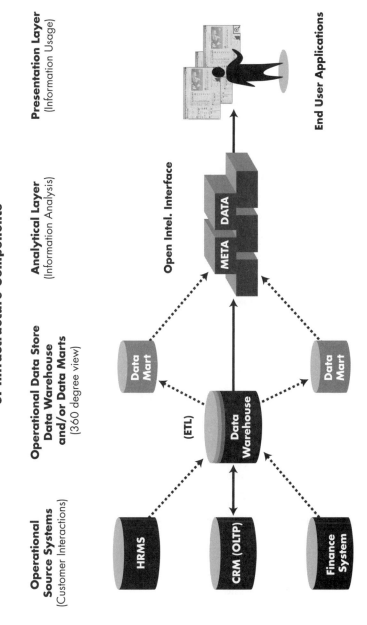

Operational Source Systems (Customer Interactions)

Operational Data Store Data Warehouse and/or Data Marts (360 degree view)

Analytical Layer (Information Analysis)

Presentation Layer (Information Usage)

HRMS

CRM (OLTP)

Finance System

(ETL)

Data Warehouse

Data Mart

Data Mart

Open Intel. Interface

META DATA

End User Applications

refocusing efforts to create executive cockpits, dashboards, and score-cards using portal and database technologies or new packaged applications that look similar to the traditional executive-information systems.

These management tools focus on the delivery of the key metrics and specific information needed to evaluate the state of the business at a glance, rather than requiring cobbled-together information from several different reports and sources. The features of these applications typically include:

- Graphical and metaphorical representations of critical areas of the business (e.g., sales, service, marketing, etc.) with key metrics that drive that function—for example, customer-segment metrics, sales conversion, marketing performance, or product line revenue and profitability.

- One-click navigation that drills down or expands to retrieve more information.

- Personalization of the user interface so users can arrange the information and view only what they want.

- Subscription functionality that lets users ask to be notified of changes and be sent new information as it becomes available in the form of reports, emails, and notifications.

- Search capabilities that allow users to ask questions like, "Is there a specific report that shows me customer service metrics from last year?"

- Access to unstructured information that gives color to hard metrics like procedures, policies, emails, or marketing creative materials.

Business performance management is a process that allows individuals from all levels of the organization to review key performance drivers, evaluate specific strategies, and review key processes at a glance. Most organizations create these applications at the executive level so they can track key performance indicators of the corporate strategy. Then, analysts can use the CI infrastructure described in the previous section to drill down to access more detail.

Organizations that have become proficient at creating dashboards drive the applications down to the front lines of the organization, giving more levels of management access to key performance metrics. These applications allow frontline managers to adjust quickly to changes in the marketplace, modifications in customer behavior, or an internal change in performance.

Stage 3: Decision Enablement through Automation

As shown, Stages 1 and 2 of the customer-intelligence roadmap provide information and reports regarding the events and activities in the business. The next stage is the application of automation tools that help in facilitating a decision, or evaluating the decision once it has been made. For example, if it is found that customer churn has increased by one percent in the previous two months, a natural next step might be to ask when this last happened, what actions were taken, and whether or not they worked.

Although it may seem simple, most organizations have not captured much data about the decisions they have made, the actions taken, and the results achieved. Even though few companies have compiled much of a knowledge base around decisions, it is possible to implement processes and technologies to capture relevant information and, by so doing, greatly enhance quality and speed of decision making. SC Johnson Wax, for example, implemented such a system within its commercialization process. This area of the business was responsible for all of the activities involved in bringing a newly developed product to market—from prototype through to packaging. By defining the hundreds of typical decisions required from design to delivery, and by using a custom-designed tool to capture the decision-making stages, the firm was able to build a database of historical decisions and relate them to marketplace results.

The following steps help to create a decision-enablement infrastructure:

1. Identify key issues and metrics for given processes.

2. Develop business rules defined by subject matter experts that help to systematically recommend a course of action at each decision point.

3. Create dashboards to view and monitor the driving metrics and key issues.

4. Leverage alert functionality so that decision makers are proactively notified when certain metrics go over or under identified thresholds. An example alert might be, "Show sales velocity over time and let me know when our average sales cycle increases to two months." Or "Let me know when any of our top 20 customers drop 2 percent in profitability."

5. Generate a mechanism that enables decision makers to research the recommendation, including who came up with the answer,

how well it worked, how many times it worked, details of the action plan, and what the other alternatives are. In order to provide this type of information, the use of structured information (rows, columns, metrics, etc.) needs to be combined with unstructured information (procedures, policies, emails, documents, etc.).

6. Produce a tool that documents the course of action taken.

7. Introduce a mechanism for evaluating and capturing the results of the action taken.

The decision–enablement process is summarized in Exhibit 4.5.

Exhibit 4.5
Decision-Enablement Process

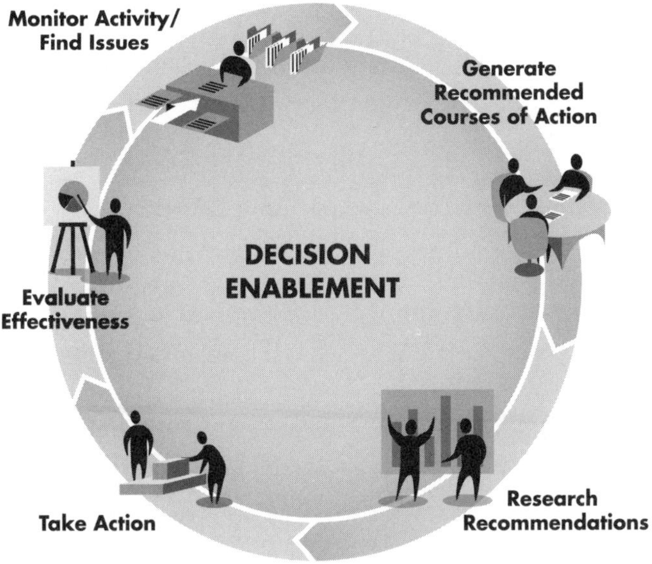

Stage 4: Business Activity Monitoring

Business activity monitoring (BAM) refers to the decision-enablement process when it is implemented within a real-time environment and supported by a technology infrastructure. Instead of relying on proactive monitoring of dashboards, real-time alerts notify the right people when certain thresholds are reached.

As the pace of innovation increases, customer expectations continue to rise, supply chains become ever more streamlined, and the need for immediate notification of specific events is growing. Increasingly, companies need this information as it becomes available so that they can react immediately to solve issues or evaluate opportunities.

Examples of how BAM is used include:

- Sophisticated customer service organizations that can balance staff allocation to react to peaks and valleys in inbound customer inquiries.

- Supply chains that monitor parts en route and can adjust production and shipping schedules based on late and early arrival of components.

- Homeland security systems using BAM concepts to react to incoming reports, traffic patterns, and monitoring of suspects.

- Financial institutions and healthcare companies monitoring transactions in order to avoid fraudulent claims or exchanges.

Customer insight processes and infrastructure allow companies to stay in tune with customers and better anticipate their future needs. This continuous feedback allows organizations to improve the value being delivered to customers, and in ways that bolster their strategic advantages.

Key Points

- Companies tend to be poor at systematically capturing and analyzing customer data.

- Customer insight should be treated as a science, not an art. Formal processes can and should be implemented.

- A consolidated customer data infrastructure must be built, along with predictive value models and capabilities for analyzing data.

- Surveying customers and analyzing how they use your product or service leads to understanding of current needs as well as potential future needs.

- Insights generate hypotheses about new ways of doing things and these should be tested, measured, and adopted where appropriate.

- By understanding the business and technology components involved, companies can follow a roadmap to successfully implement a functional customer insight infrastructure.

Notes

1. Michael Lewis, *Moneyball: The Art of Winning an Unfair Game*. New York: W.W. Norton & Company, 2003.

2. Christina Binkley, "Lucky Numbers: Casino Chain Mines Data on Its Gamblers, and Strikes Pay Dirt; 'Secret Recipe' Lets Harrah's Target Its Low-Rollers at the Individual Level; A Free-Meal 'Intervention'," *The Wall Street Journal*, May 4, 2000 p. A1.

3. Christina Binkley, "Lucky Numbers."

4. Rajiv Lal and Patricia Martone Carrolo, *Harrah's Entertainment Inc.*, #9-502-011. Boston: Harvard Business School Press, May 22, 2002.

5. Lal and Carrolo, *Harrah's Entertainment Inc.*

6. Clayton M. Christensen, *The Innovator's Dilemma: When New Technologies Cause Great Firms to Fail.* Boston: Harvard Business School Press, June 1997.

7. Robert M. Grant, *Contemporary Strategy Analysis: Concepts, Techniques, Applications, 4th Edition.* Oxford, UK: Blackwell Publishers, 2002.

8. Carton Donofrio Partners, "W.L. Gore & Associates, Inc. Case Study," *www.cartondonofrio.com/clients/casestudies.cfm?%20action= detail&doc_id=58,* available as of December 10, 2003.

9. Grant, *Contemporary Strategy Analysis: Concepts, Techniques, Applications.*

10. Stefan Thomke, "R&D Comes to Services: Bank of America's Pathbreaking Experiments," *Harvard Business Review,* #R0304E. Boston: Harvard Business School Press, March 2003.

11. David Rosenblum, Doug Tomlinson, and Larry Scott, "Bottom Feeding for Blockbuster Business," *Harvard Business Review,* #R0303C. Boston: Harvard Business School Press, March 2003.

CHAPTER
5

Demand Visibility and Response

Most companies are poor forecasters of demand levels and patterns. As a result, they limit long-term profitability by hampering their ability to innovate and capture new business, and also dampen short-term profits by failing to detect and respond effectively to current levels and types of demand.

In Chapter 4, we discussed the customer insight processes that help firms deepen their understanding of customers, detect emerging marketplace needs, and carve out long-term profit growth. In this chapter, we look beyond customer insight and at the wider demand picture. We focus on demand forecasting and response processes that are critical to detecting and responding to current demand levels. Unfortunately, most managers adopt defective forecasting methods or simply believe that effective forecasting is too complex due to the highly dynamic nature of the market. That misconception leads to unsound assumptions regarding future demand levels, limited consensus on where the market is going, and lack of coordination across the firm in response to the marketplace. Companies then have inadequate ability to respond to areas of weak demand—or capitalize on strong demand—leading to difficulty in correctly projecting and optimizing revenue and earnings levels for the organization as a whole.[1]

As discussed in earlier chapters, successful organizations have clear and focused strategies but they also complement these with excellent responsiveness to ongoing fluctuations in demand and customer needs. These organizations maintain high levels of visibility into demand conditions by constantly monitoring the external environment. High visibility into market, customer, and demand conditions enables leading firms to shore up areas of weak demand and capitalize on new opportunities quickly. Insight into demand changes and variations in the behavior of the customer base allows companies to configure products and services to boost revenue and profitability. Furthermore, strong demand visibility allows firms to fine-tune inventory levels, resource levels and assignments, budgets, and investment plans in order to optimize execution in the market and boost revenue and profits.

Our research measured the responsiveness of companies in many industries by tracking consistency of profitability. For example, during the same period, Compaq's profitability fluctuated far more than Dell's. When Dell sees a drop in demand, it is better able to lower cost levels. Similarly, Dell was able to capitalize on islands of strong demand for items like printers, servers, and back-to-school PCs during a generally weak business environment. In addition, when demand surges, Dell ramps up quickly to meet it. By contrast, Compaq's profitability suffered significantly during periods of both low and high demand. A similar picture emerges when comparing Wal-Mart with K-Mart, Abbott Laboratories with Pfizer, and Southwest with United. Dell, Wal-Mart, Abbott, and Southwest fully understand the demand picture, quickly deploy resources against it, and adjust expenditures to match realistic revenue projections.

In addition, visibility into customer needs leads to insight into emerging demand areas and provides vital information to the product development teams. This allows for fine tuning of R&D budgets and the overall operations of the firm.

Demand visibility and customer insight are the operational linchpins of all successful companies. And when joined with a sound strategy, the triad leads to enduring business success.

Demand Visibility

Successful companies carefully monitor current demand levels and apply quantitative frameworks to make short-range projections. Firms such as Dell, HP, and Wal-Mart are able to produce very accurate short-term demand projections that are the operational lifeblood of these organizations. Resource, product, budget, and pricing decisions are all driven by these projections.

For example, Wal-Mart tracks daily sales of all products in two-year periods. Through its RetailLink system, it communicates this data to its supplier base. Suppliers can see how daily sales are trending versus previous periods and make realistic projections of monthly and quarterly demand for their products or services. This type of data is called a time-series and provides the basis for a wide variety of statistical projections that help companies gear operations to meet market demand. Time-series forecasting is, by far, the most common method for understanding the short-term demand picture in most industries. Companies such as HP have invested significantly in improving their forecasting capabilities. For example, they have developed methods that adjust time-series data based on the position of a product in its life cycle. For technology products in particular, the product life cycle is rapid but often follows a distinct pattern. For such a product, projecting future demand from current daily sales may be misleading, as many technology products start slowly and ramp up explosively before quickly commoditizing.

In the interest of forecasting accurately, HP has developed typical profiles based on actual historical sales data for similar types of products. The information helps HP predict the inflection points in demand that accompany a product's lifecycle.[2]

Receiving an accurate demand picture is the key to successful operations. For example, anticipating the ramp-up and down in demand for a new printer allows manufacturing and fulfillment to plan appropriately. A demand-based ramp-up prevents inventory shortfalls and lost sales, and a timely ramp-down averts inventory gluts and expensive write-offs. Most companies resort to straight-line projections based on current conditions or guesswork when it comes to projecting demand. Unfortunately, this approach nearly always damages the bottom line.

Most successful firms use actual sales and historical patterns to make short-term projections. They may also augment these approaches with market-testing approaches to monitor short-term demand for products. Zara, the highly successful European fashion retailer, combines rapid product-development cycles and pilot-market launches to gauge demand for new products. Whereas most retailers take three to six months to design and launch a new product, Zara completes the task in three to six weeks. They have configured their design, manufacturing, and fulfillment processes to execute on these revolutionary concept-to-rack cycle times. This allows them to test market new products and respond quicker with new or refined designs. Zara, through its market-driven approach, gains an intimate feel for current demand in the highly fickle fashion world.[3]

Best Practices for Increased Visibility

Most managers believe accurate forecasting is extremely difficult, if not impossible. However, many companies such as Wal-Mart, Walgreen's, HP, and IBM consistently produce accurate forecasts and healthy margins. Accurate, market-driven forecasting separates these market leaders from the others. Most companies base forecasts on the judgments of managers and salespeople. Field-level people are considered to have better insight because they are close to the action. However, many studies have shown that these forecasts are inaccurate and relying on them leads to suboptimal decisions for the firm. Salespeople generally produce forecasts that are remarkably similar to their quotas— in most cases a triumph of hope over reality. Managers are under tremendous pressure to produce results and often inject too much optimism into their projections.[4]

Finally, people throughout the organization have varying degrees of market exposure, experience, and optimism. Combining these opinions and hoping for an accurate forecast is unrealistic.

Demand-driven companies have standardized the process. As shown in Exhibit 5.1, they generally follow a set of guidelines associated with sound forecasting:

- *Standardize inputs.* These companies ensure that field personnel use similar rules-based standards for classifying data so that human bias is limited.

123

Exhibit 5.1
Defining a Process for Forecasting Accurately

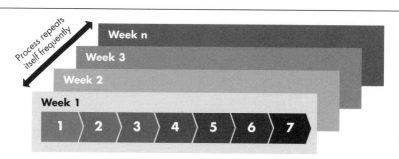

1 Rigorous rules guide the collection of facts by salespeople close to customers.

2 Facts are rolled up automatically to finance department where they become part of a time-series.

3 Finance applies a statistical correction factor based on previous numbers for similar periods.

4 Single statistical forecast drives all planning—judgments limited.

5 No "back-up" forecasts or plans are permitted.

6 Budgets aligned with single forecast on a weekly basis . . . Resources released in waves.

7 Planning sessions are cross departmental.

- *Standardize models.* Most successful companies utilize the time-series model, as shown in Exhibit 5.2, for conducting forecasts. This compares current projections to past projections and associated actual outcomes. The resulting simple statistical methods produce surprisingly accurate projections.

- *Ensure frequency and granularity.* The best companies run projections frequently, such as every day or weekly. They also ensure that projections are produced for as many product lines and business areas as possible. Without granularity, little effective decision making can result.

Exhibit 5.2
Forecasting Time-Series Model

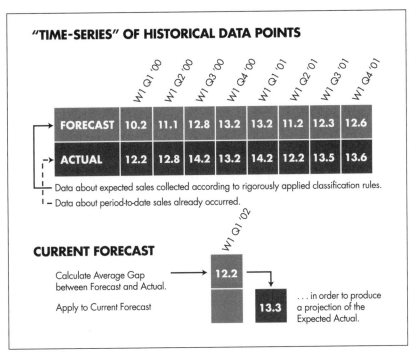

"TIME-SERIES" OF HISTORICAL DATA POINTS

	W1 Q1 '00	W1 Q2 '00	W1 Q3 '00	W1 Q4 '00	W1 Q1 '01	W1 Q2 '01	W1 Q3 '01	W1 Q4 '01
FORECAST	10.2	11.1	12.8	13.2	13.2	11.2	12.3	12.6
ACTUAL	12.2	12.8	14.2	13.2	14.2	12.2	13.5	13.6

– Data about expected sales collected according to rigorously applied classification rules.
– Data about period-to-date sales already occurred.

CURRENT FORECAST

W1 Q1 '02

Calculate Average Gap
between Forecast and Actual. → 12.2

Apply to Current Forecast → 13.3 . . . in order to produce
a projection of the
Expected Actual.

- *Measure forecast performance.* By monitoring the accuracy of forecast results, the time-series projections can be made more accurate. Measurement also points to areas of the forecast process that require improvement.

Responding to Market Demand

Gaining visibility is the first step taken by successful companies in optimizing profitability through operations. The second is ensuring the organization responds quickly and efficiently to the information.

Most modern organizations are made up of distinct business units and subsidiaries of acquired organizations. Obtaining a unified and optimized response in such a complex system is extremely challenging. At IBM, the regular weekly meeting convenes all major areas to synchronize supply and demand—that is, to agree on what is selling well and how much to build, and to discuss plans to bolster areas that are struggling through promotions and pricing changes.

The key process for balancing supply and demand within most organizations is *sales and operations planning (S&OP)*. During this process, the key demand-side and supply-side executives convene with forecasters to assess the various actions required to optimize supply and demand. This leads to:

- A profile of demand levels by product and area.

- Agreed-upon demand stimulation activities.

- Revised production and fulfillment schedules.

- Consistent resource deployment and budgeting refinements.

Gaining demand visibility and coordinating the firm's response are not just sales and marketing tasks. In successful organizations, every function throughout the firm is organized to be demand responsive. Too often, silos of policies and processes develop within the various functions of an organization, and decision making is not aligned to the marketplace. The goal of the demand-responsive organization is to ensure every function operates with customer needs and demand levels as its highest priority. Functional managers must be prepared to quickly redeploy resources and change priorities and budgets to better respond to the market. The following are examples of the areas within each function that are impacted by changes in demand:

- *Finance.*

  Company earnings projections vary based on revenue forecast and investment decisions. Business unit revenue and budgets, as well as department budgets vary based on revenue forecasts.

- *Product development.*

  Long-term R&D is adjusted if market insight indicates areas of emerging demand. Short-term product development budgets and efforts are refined if emerging demand indicates new products or product configurations.

- *Manufacturing and fulfillment.*

  Factory capacity, parts ordering, inventory levels, and distribution capacity are all dependent on projected demand levels in the marketplace.

- *Sales and marketing.*

  Sales and marketing must develop revenue management tactics to counter areas of weak demand, as well as quickly communicate strong demand opportunities to the rest of the organization.

- *Top management.*

  Overall earnings and cash-flow projections, new product plans, and acquisition strategies are often impacted by surprising turns in demand. The closer top management is to current market and demand conditions, the earlier it knows of changes and the more time it has to respond.

- *Across business units.*

  Business units often contain many of the functions listed above. All must be adjusted to demand levels experienced by the business unit. In addition, shared services organizations must adjust resources and capacity to align with varying demand across the business units.

- *With suppliers and other value system partners.*

  Sharing demand information with other companies in the value system leads to faster fulfillment of company needs, and healthier partnerships.

There are three major factors affecting successful responsiveness to demand:

1. The ability to shore up areas of weak demand through revenue-management techniques.

2. The significant affect of a firm's pricing approaches on profitability.

3. The importance of cross-enterprise collaboration and accountability in implementing a responsive approach to demand changes.

Best Practices for Demand Responsiveness

Responding to demand patterns requires a consistent outlook, constant consensus building, and careful coordination. We have observed the following Best Practices among those organizations that respond effectively to demand:

- *Frequent meeting of key demand- and supply-side executives with forecasters.*

  Projections and the implications for supply, demand, and finance are assessed on a weekly or daily basis.

- *Full senior-level commitment and involvement.*

  Meetings should not be delegated. The demand picture is the primary influencer of all major resource, capacity, and budgetary decisions and senior management needs to be there to hear it and coordinate the action.

- *Constant and consistent collaboration across departments.*

  All areas must be involved in the process. Not all will participate enthusiastically at first, but success relies on building confidence and consensus over time in the interest of achieving unified visibility and coordinated response.

- *A high degree of investment in the forecast process to build trust.*

  Forecast models become more accurate as inputs are standardized and historical data builds. Continual investment is required over multiple years to build a world-class forecasting model.

- *Measurement of team members on coordinated action.*

  It is essential for the organization to regularly develop and collaborate on a company-wide game plan and follow up with swift and coordinated action.

Exhibit 5.3 outlines some key questions to begin to understand where a firm stands in its ability to respond effectively to marketplace demand.

Exhibit 5.3
Forecasting and Planning Evaluation Checklist

FORECASTING EVALUATION CHECKLIST

	YES	NO
• Do facts collected under rigorous rules guide the inputs to your forecasting process?	☐	☐
• Are opportunities for biases of manager/ salespeople kept out of your forecasting process?	☐	☐
• Is a lengthy time-series of data used for comparison when arriving at your final forecast?	☐	☐
• Do managers throughout your organization put a high degree of trust and confidence in your forecasting process?	☐	☐
• Is your forecast updated frequently?	☐	☐
• Does your process allow you to "hit your numbers" on a regular basis?		

PLANNING EVALUATION CHECKLIST

	YES	NO
• Is all the planning activity in your organization tied to one single forecast?	☐	☐
• Are plans throughout the organization prepared using common assumptions?	☐	☐
• Is technology used effectively in your planning process to increase its speed and effectiveness?	☐	☐
• Are resources held or released dynamically according to the latest forecast?	☐	☐
• Are managers closest to the customer able to make timely inputs to the planning process guided by rigorous rules and templates?	☐	☐

How much opportunity are you missing because of poor forecasting and planning?

Science of Revenue Management

Most organizations periodically implement demand-stimulation activities such as new promotions or special incentives for the sales force. However, these activities are often not well planned or statistically based, and no consistent methodology or understanding of expected outcomes is in place. Marketing and sales will tend to exaggerate the effect of these activities and, instead of assessing historical success rates, companies will rely on the judgment of campaign or sales managers, leading to unrealistic expectations. In addition, these efforts are usually not coordinated properly with manufacturing and fulfillment operations.

In recent years, some leading retailers have had success following the example of the airlines in developing sophisticated and effective revenue-management policies, techniques, and technologies. Zara, for example, tracks all historic promotional and discounting activities and uses this data to provide realistic predictions of the outcome of revenue-management activities. Zara's database and revenue-management discipline allows it to apply promotions and discounts on a daily basis at an item and store level. This technique is far more reflective of the granularity of demand in the fashion retail industry.[5]

Most organizations are underskilled and underinvested in revenue management. Discipline and process for assessing good techniques and expected outcomes are not in place in most marketing organizations. These efforts are a black box to the rest of the organization that must take optimistic projections based on face value, apply a discount based on gut feel, or await an uncertain outcome. This approach does not allow the organization to allocate inventory, plan capacity, deploy resources, or set budgets in the appropriate manner. In addition, top management does not have a clear picture of the likely revenue outcome, making earnings projections and cash-flow planning more difficult.

Power of Pricing

Most organizations also have poor pricing strategies. They generally and unnecessarily underprice through a series of planned price breaks for various customers compounded with discretionary discounting by the sales force and after-the-fact rebates. This has a cascading effect that significantly erodes the original sales price. Our research shows that it is not unusual for the realized price to be over 30 percent below list price and for the variation between the highest and lowest realized price for the same product to be well over 50 percent. In addition, most firms do not adequately track realized prices and don't have good visibility into the extent of their pricing problems.

Pricing discipline in which rules are established and followed across the organization is the most important aspect of sound pricing strategy. In addition, pricing changes, discounts, and rebates should be tracked as thoroughly as sales price in order to generate a full picture of the firm's realized prices. Investing in a pricing and tracking strategy leads to higher profitability for the firm.

The great demand-driven companies focus on forecasting and response. Accurate projections and coordinated reaction allows them to shore up struggling areas and target emerging demand opportunities more effectively. In doing so, they create a virtuous circle. Early warning avoids spending time on firefighting caused by missed earnings and cash-flow problems. This approach frees up resources that capitalize on opportunities that have become clearer through improved visibility.

Key Points

- Successful companies are tuned in to changes in the pattern of demand and leverage this visibility to make better planning and execution decisions.

- The ability to respond quickly and flexibly to changes in the profile and level of demand is a hallmark of great companies.

- Companies should also invest in better revenue management and pricing to better stimulate revenue and optimize profitability.

Notes

1. Philip Bligh, Darius Vaskelis, and John Kelleher, "Taking The Frenzy Out of Forecasting," *Optimize*, Issue 17, March 2003, *www.optimizemag.com/issue/017/financial.htm*, available as of February 3, 2004.

2. Jim Burruss and Dorothea Kuettner, "Forecasting for Short-lived Products: Hewlett-Packard's Journey," *The Journal of Business Forecasting Methods and Systems*, Volume 21, Number 4, pp. 9–17. Flushing, NY: Institute of Business Forecasting, Winter 2002–2003.

3. Pankaj Ghemawat and Jose Luis Nueno, *ZARA: Fast Fashion*, #9-703-497. Boston: Harvard Business School Press, April 1, 2003.

4. Dan Lovallo and Daniel Kahneman, "Delusions of Success: How Optimism Undermines Executives' Decisions," *Harvard Business Review*, #R0307D. Boston: Harvard Business School Press, July 1, 2003.

5. Ghemawat and Nueno, *ZARA: Fast Fashion*.

CHAPTER
6

An Enterprise-Wide Approach to CRM

Few companies provide seamless customer interactions across departments. In fact, it is usually the opposite. In most companies, customer orders or requests are routed through many departments, including sales, finance, billing, manufacturing, and customer service. As client calls are transferred from person to person, and information bounces around departments, departmental rules often trump the desire to provide swift and seamless service. In addition, too little attention is given to the differences in customer needs or importance to the firm. We find a tendency among most managers to be too internally focused and departmentally minded, rather than customer-minded. As a result, their employees are usually unaware of the priorities attached to various customer interactions. So customers tend to get treated in uniform, often-shoddy ways, making most companies difficult to do business with.

Leading companies break down departmental barriers and manage customer relationships holistically. Cross-departmental collaboration is encouraged and the importance of customer priorities and activities supersede most other departmental issues.

For example, in implementing their CRM initiative, PepsiAmericas developed a coordinated enterprise-wide approach. The company first acknowledged that each of its three identified customer segments had different service, delivery, and relationship needs. Rather than create a uniform approach to customer interaction that would serve no one group optimally, PepsiAmericas assessed the types of dealings and processes that provided the greatest value to each segment, and developed specific approaches for each one.[1] This type of strategic customer segmentation dictates what kinds of treatments each group receives, which in turn drives policy, process, and behavior across the entire organization.

In reality, each department within your firm significantly affects value delivered to customers, and it is the responsibility of each department to deliver unique and satisfying service to customers. Each department already has a *functional strategy* that defines its operating plans and budgets. But in most organizations there is no equivalent *customer strategy*, that is, no *central definition of customer policy and interdepartmental process related to customer interactions*. To optimize value delivered to customers and the costs associated with it, companies must take a more customer-centric approach to defining operational plans across departments.

Functional planning, policies, and operational priorities at companies like Dell, PepsiAmericas, and Harrah's are driven from goals associated with addressing customer segments. In these companies, customer goals drive departmental planning, which leads to better coordination and monitoring of customer activity across the firm.

We recommend that, in addition to functional strategy, your company should also create a *customer strategy* that coordinates the specific treatments and metrics associated with creating and delivering optimal value for specific customers and customer segments. Like DNA code, customer strategy provides to every department the instructions on how to meet each customer's needs. Rather than relying on each department to get customer policies and processes right on its own, the customer strategy defines an integrated set of customer processes and policies across all parts of the enterprise. Your *customer strategy* must ensure that segments are treated uniquely, the customer experience is coordinated across your enterprise, and customer insight processes are integrated into daily operations.

What Is Customer Strategy and How Does It Help?

Customer strategy helps avoid the silo effect that exists among departments in many organizations. As said above, customer strategy encourages department managers and employees to think first about the customer and second about departmental policies. For example, finance departments usually define credit rules and payment terms that provide optimal risk management and daily sales outstanding (DSO) metrics for the firm. Although basic ground rules must exist, top customers likely should also have their own tailored credit rules and payment terms designed to make it easy for them to do business with the company.

Customer strategy must drive customer-related policy; existing departmental rules are secondary in importance. The same goes for internally focused inventory policy and fulfillment rules that fail to put the customer first. In many organizations, departments become fiefdoms and lose sight of their mission to support the delivery of value to customers. By contrast, high performance firms breach the walls between departments.

How Customer Strategy Relates to Corporate and Functional Strategy

When properly defined, customer strategy derives from corporate- or business-unit strategy, and integrates seamlessly with functional strategies across departments. However, "strategy" tends to be an overused business term; therefore, we should define our use of the term. To illustrate this point, let's examine the various types of strategy that are deployed at a large company like General Electric. GE's *corporate strategy* is its highest-level strategy; it defines the portfolio of businesses the company competes in and includes general guidelines on how each unit should be run and what results are expected. For example, GE's corporate head office insists on the application of standard management training and practices to each business. It also demands Six Sigma quality across all operations, and sells businesses that are not number one or two in their industries. Using this system, GE's various business units compete in a wide variety of industries, including financial services, aircraft engines, appliances, medical systems, and media.

However, GE's corporate strategy does not stipulate how individual businesses will compete against industry rivals. In order to determine the competitive positioning for each business unit, strategies that describe the prospective scope and advantage in each market are defined. We refer to these as *business unit* or *competitive strategies*. Furthermore, each business unit is run fairly autonomously and has its own functional departments, such as sales, marketing, finance, operations, procurement, and customer service. The corporate and competitive strategies are translated into action plans for each department through *functional strategies*, which usually consist of regularly updated operating plans and budgets.

This is the typical interrelation of strategies within most large corporations as depicted in Exhibit 6.1.

Clearly, competitive and functional strategies are intrinsically linked. Functional strategies are derived from competitive strategy, and help define how the competitive strategy (i.e., low cost or differentiation) is implemented in the policies and processes in each area of the firm. Unfortunately, functional strategies are often inadequate because they don't gather and coordinate the diverse customer interactions across the firm in ways that deliver consistent and differentiated experiences to customers.

Exhibit 6.1
Strategy Interrelation at Most Large Firms

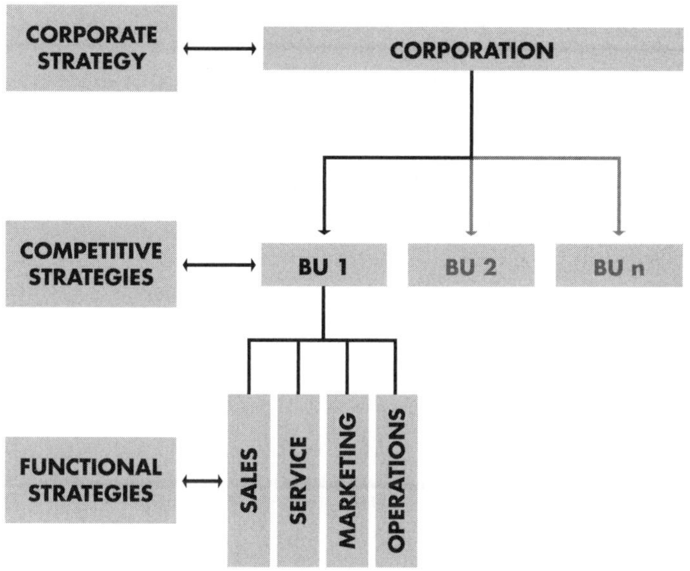

Source: Robert M. Grant, *Contemporary Strategy Analysis*, Blackwell Publishers, 4th edition, January 2002.

A *customer strategy* can provide the customer-specific guidelines required for each function. Customer strategy helps marshal the critical customer-related activities and processes throughout the business. It consists of instructions for each functional area of the business on how they should treat each customer segment or individual customer. Just as firms seek to build competitive advantage into each activity across all departments, customer strategy helps define an additional level of tailoring at the customer level that provides even deeper differentiation, fit, and protection against imitation by rivals.

In summary, the key goals for a customer strategy are:

- *Marshal customer-related activities.*

  Ensure that each department adopts policies and carries out activities in an integrated way that is designed to provide seamless, "easy to do business with" service to each customer.

- *Coordinate differential treatments.*

  Ensure that each customer segment receives uniquely tailored service in ways that support the growth goals for these customer groups and strengthens the firm's competitive advantages.

- *Define formal customer-management processes.*

  Ensure that customer-performance goals are set and measured and incentive plans across all levels and roles reflect customer goals. Also, ensure that customer data is captured, analyzed, and shared across the organization.

Similar to GE's corporate strategy, high-level customer strategy guidelines may exist at the corporate level. However, customer strategy is typically implemented at the business-unit level (unless business units share customers). Exhibit 6.2 shows how customer strategy interrelates to strategy within a typical large organization.

Key Components of an Effective Customer Strategy

Customer strategy ties together customer priorities and policies across traditional functional strategies. It helps the firm seamlessly deliver optimum value and monitor performance with its most valuable customers. By formalizing customer strategy, the firm can maximize value delivered for each segment, gain visibility into investment and effort levels for each segment, and track customer–related

Exhibit 6.2
Introducing Customer Strategy

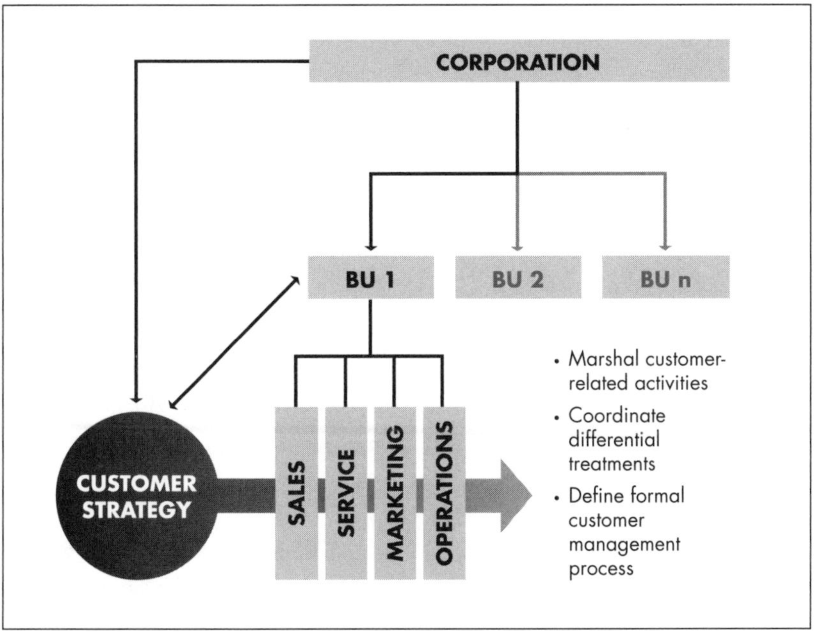

performance levels for all areas of the firm. In this section, we examine the typical components you'd expect to find in an effective customer strategy:

- Customer segmentation and tailored service

- Organization and coordination

- Customer interaction plan

- Performance management

Customer Segmentation and Tailored Service

Customer policy and process is usually defined by segment. Traditionally, marketing strategy defines customer segmentation goals and go-to-market approaches associated with each customer segment. Segmentation may already be fully defined in marketing plans and may not need to be incorporated with the customer strategy. However, most marketing strategies do not fully define segmentation and more detail is often needed.

Once segmentation is reviewed or defined in more detail, the unique treatments for each segment must be defined. This step typically requires policy and process changes throughout the firm and the implementation must be highly coordinated. The key to customer loyalty is the ability to properly understand customer needs and value and then to translate those into specific service levels and interactions that are tailored to each customer. For cost leaders, for example, a subset of customers may not need high levels of service or other factors deemed important by another subset of customers. In a case like this, the firm may be able to reduce overall cost by serving less-demanding customers more cheaply. A key to creating value for customers is to locate connections between your value chain and the customer's. Returning to an earlier example, Dell learned that its customers spend significant time and effort managing their PC assets. For the convenience of some of its customers, Dell staff is sometimes placed inside the customer's operations and is responsible for managing these tasks. For businesses where this approach makes sense, powerful customer insight is delivered.

At the same time, tailoring adds cost, and firms must determine whether the cost exceeds the expected price premiums or cost savings.

When profitably achieved, tailoring creates competitive advantage for the firm. It raises switching costs for the customer, as they must give up benefits to switch to rivals. Tailored service also creates an emotional attachment to your brand and can be used as a tool to help defray price pressure as core products and services commoditize over time.

Finally, rivals inevitably adapt to even the most innovative organizations. Tailoring customer operations and service levels is an ongoing process that helps gain and retain a competitive edge.

Organization and Coordination

To offset the internal, product-centric mentality that besets many organizations, some have made the decision to overhaul their organizational structure to be more formally aligned by customer segment. For example, in the past 3M was made up of 34 business units that were defined based on the products made and sold by those units. The company discovered that each business unit often sold to the same customers and little consolidated insight was shared across the organizations. 3M decided to create seven market-facing business units based on various types of customers. Now each of the product units goes to market through the customer units.[2]

There is a spectrum of choices as to how a firm organizes its P&L business units and its go-to-market approach. Some structures are far more customer-centric than others. Organizations with complex products and few shared customers across product lines are more likely to be organized around product lines. Companies with many shared customers, services firms, or those with frequently changing product lines, are likely to veer toward more formal customer-centric approaches. Across the spectrum there is a range of options and no single right answer for all organizations. However, we have found that most firms need to shift along the spectrum toward a more customer-centric structure. This tends to create a more outward facing culture, and clearly signals the importance of the customer throughout the firm. It also focuses the organization on driving business with certain customers, and creates greater accountability to customer performance goals.

In addition to defining organizational decisions, across-the-firm customer strategy helps identify and coordinate the policies and processes required by the segmentation and tailored service approaches. Each area of the firm plays a part—however small—in the customer's experience. When customer experiences are adapted for each customer or segment, the policies and processes in each part of the firm must be adjusted to support them.

Returning to our Dell example, we have described how Dell's best corporate customers receive higher levels of service, and that, in some cases, Dell loads the customer's proprietary software on the machines and tests it before shipping.

This initiative requires unique manufacturing processes for these choice customers. A high-speed network was installed in the factory to quickly load software onto the machines during assembly. Obviously, this process also requires very specific technical instructions from buyers, additional software experts on staff, special pricing and billing instructions, and processes for procuring the customer's proprietary software and its frequent updates. Many aspects of Dell's overall business are involved in these activities. All functions must be carefully coordinated to ensure that each activity is configured for each type of customer.

Clearly, activities in one area of the business are closely linked with activities in another. For example, reducing high after-sales servicing costs at Xerox was eventually achieved not through efficient breakthroughs in servicing, but by redesigning copiers and parts to ease diagnostics and replacement. This holistic, coordinated approach is essential to the delivery of seamless and unique experiences to customers.

Customer Interaction Plan

The customer strategy includes definitions of channel architecture, customer touch-points, escalation procedures, customer ownership, and other interactions across the customer lifecycle. The functional strategies produced by various departments may already address certain aspects of customer interactions. However, typically the specifications are not complete or consistent with other departmental plans. Customer strategy must coordinate these interaction-related policies, processes, and any other directives to ensure that a consistent and coordinated approach is in place across the enterprise. Often, the firm will have specific goals associated with certain customer segments as a result of customer segment and value analysis. For example, it may wish to increase or reduce the volume of business done with certain customers through certain channels. Customer strategy ensures these goals are communicated throughout the enterprise so that appropriate effort and investment is applied to the right interactions.

In one example, the PC unit of Toshiba learned from analyzing business and consumer surveys that customers perceived little difference between rival products that were currently on the market. Instead, these customers were placing more value on services such as ease of purchase and custom configuration. To address this change in customer priorities, Toshiba created a company-wide customer strategy that focused on providing easy-to-use direct channels to customers. Rather than *pushing* products on customers, they created a *pull* strategy that facilitated closer customer connections. In order to implement the revised *customer strategy*, Toshiba made significant investments in direct channels, such as the Internet, as well as changes in the firm's organizational structure and its supply chain.

Toshiba used an information system to ensure consistent and accurate information across all customer touch-points and also developed predictive models to project demand and customer behavior. The company believes that the new customer and channel strategy improves its ability to sell its products and services. It also now has better financial controls due to better revenue projections and process efficiencies.

Performance Management

Given the investments required to implement a more tailored and integrated customer approach, it makes sense to take a formal approach in meeting customer goals. For example, in a recent meeting we had with a Fortune 500 company, many of the executives were at first convinced that the firm was doing a good job monitoring customer-related goals. However, outside of overall revenue, not a single customer-related metric was presented in the quarterly management reviews of each business unit. This is not uncommon. Unfortunately, many companies do not set formal customer performance goals and do not focus on customer-related metrics during management review meetings.

To properly track performance, management reviews should prominently feature metrics such as:

- Customer acquisition versus goals per segment

- New product/service adoption versus goals per segment

- Percent change in revenue per period per segment/customer

- Percent change in profitability per period per segment/customer

- Service level performance (turnaround time, delivery time, defects, service call on-time, etc.) per segment/customer versus goals

What gets measured usually gets done, and a formal approach to measuring customer performance is required to make it happen.

Enterprise Marketing Management: How Customer Strategy Integrates with Marketing Strategy

In this chapter, we have seen how a customer strategy can help marshal and coordinate customer activities across every function of the firm. When implemented successfully, it enables companies to carefully define and consistently deliver tailored experiences to each customer segment, or even each individual customer. In many ways, the objectives of customer strategy overlap with the traditional objectives of the marketing department—especially around defining and ensuring consistent experiences for customers. Marketing's goal is to help the organization profitably sell more products. While doing this, it should help to build strong brands and achieve a healthy portfolio of products and services within desirable market and customer segments.

However, in most organizations, the primary marketing goal of driving sales is often diluted by a myriad of other marketing activities. We agree with mounting recent opinion that marketing plans are traditionally not focused directly enough on driving sales and not well integrated with the organization as a whole.[3] Systematic problems exist with the way marketing is currently implemented in most organizations. These include:

- *Marketing is too isolated, defining programs and policies that are not widely or fully adopted by the organization as a whole.* Executives in the marketing area do not carry sufficient clout within the executive team to properly champion the necessary policy and process changes required throughout the organization.

- *Marketing is often out of touch with the real needs of the sales force and different personality types within these functions exacerbate the rift.*

- *Marketing does not fully consider the impacts on branding and customer experience of every function of the company such as finance, operations, and HR.*

- *Marketing professionals are overly focused on the creative aspects of their jobs.* More science is needed to ensure marketing expenditures are better planned, executed, and measured. Without this, marketing cannot consistently and predictably achieve the goal of producing higher sales.

Customer strategy can help alleviate these problems by ensuring that key customer experience and brand impacts are integrated throughout the organization. Firms can successfully execute on their strategies only if their marketing plans, brand architecture, and customer strategy are closely integrated.

Consider, for example, how customer strategy and brand architecture are interwoven in the operations of Neutrogena. The company generates industry-leading profitability through a differentiated strategy that delivers a mild residue-free soap formulated for pH balance that is gentler on the skin and recommended by dermatologists. To help ensure the integrity of its skin-care brand, the soap has no perfume and only mild cleansing properties. These are trade-offs that will turn off some customers but are vital to the consistency of the brand. Delivering on these brand attributes also involves more expensive manufacturing processes—another trade-off but again one that is required to remain true to the brand. In fact, the soap is formulated, tested, manufactured, and packaged differently than other soaps. It is also marketed and distributed uniquely by using a large sales force that calls on dermatologists. The marketing approach more closely resembles that of a drug maker than a soap maker. Neutrogena advertises in medical journals, attends medical conferences, and performs research at its own skin-care institute. Every department and activity within the Neutrogena value chain is designed and configured to fulfill its mild medicinal promise.

However, in contrast to Neutrogena, many firms treat differentiation as a marketing task alone, not realizing that trust is quickly undone if any aspect of the customer experience falls short of the promise. Similarly, most CRM efforts have focused too heavily on front office issues and have fallen into the trap of under delivering on a well-marketed promise. Customer strategy helps to integrate the policy and process changes required across every customer impact point in the value chain. Similarly, marketing must be viewed as an enterprise-wide set of policies and processes. And marketing and customer strategy must be defined in lockstep.

Realistically, marketing executives rarely have the clout to change policy and processes in every department of the firm. The senior executive team must provide the leadership needed to ensure that customer experiences are coordinated across departments and are carefully structured for each customer segment.

As shown in the Neutrogena example, well-defined customer strategies can help ensure that customer-first priorities are reflected in all planning and operational decisions throughout the firm. Similarly, enterprise-wide marketing—or as some have coined it, *enterprise marketing management*—can significantly boost your brands and drive higher sales by involving all aspects of the firm in the business of selling more of your products and services. To achieve this, a systematic—even scientific—approach is needed.

The next section describes some of the key factors in implementing successful enterprise-wide marketing.[4]

Treat Marketing as a Science

Marketers have focused too much attention on the creative aspects of their work—designing advertising, developing brand image, and cooking up new campaign ideas. Creativity is vital in marketing—it is a hallmark of great marketing and vital for increasing sales. But alone it is not sufficient. More marketers need to adopt the scientific method summarized below:

- Make empirical observations and measurements of the environment (such as performance of certain segments, daily fluctuations in demand, competitive actions, trends in win rates, sales cycle lengths, speed and success of new product introductions, success of certain channels, seasonal effects, etc.).

- Develop hypotheses that fit the data and may provide enhanced performance in specific areas (e.g., pricing policy changes based on regional demand).

- Use the hypotheses to make predictions about potential improvements (e.g., average variation in regional demand decreases by 3 percent).

- Design and run experiments to test hypotheses in the marketplace.

- Measure results, adjust hypotheses, and repeat process.

This requires a different approach for most marketing functions. Companies must become systematic in implementing the scientific process. For example, they must:

- Identify the key demand-side metrics that must be tracked

- Implement the tools required to capture the metrics

- Implement policies and processes that institutionalize consistent measurement

- Implement processes for regular review and analysis of data

- Invest and assign the necessary resources to carry out these tasks

- Ensure that results become part of regular management reviews

Some marketers have tried to adopt these approaches in one form or another, but have run into roadblocks along the way. Typically they have lacked the means to gather relevant and timely marketplace information. Also, they have been faced with a lack of coordination with other areas of the organization and little knowledge of what goes on when other functions interact with customers and distributors. In addition, these efforts to adopt more scientific approaches have lacked rigor, persistence, and consistency across all areas of the business. In many cases, new capabilities must be added to the skills mix on staff. Marketing executives must increase the emphasis on the quantitative and process-oriented aspects of the marketing function.

Start by Defining and Integrating Architectures for Your Brands

When Harrah's set out on its journey to transform its brand, it started with the understanding that its fundamental marketing approach was flawed. Marketing departments based in individual properties carried out activities specific to the property and without the collective knowledge of all properties and the firm as a whole. Instead of simply hiring a marketing honcho, Harrah's CEO realized that marketing needed to become everyone's responsibility, starting with the CEO himself. A coordinated and integrated plan was needed that reflected the goals and leveraged the knowledge of the entire firm. For Harrah's that meant national rather than property-specific loyalty programs and incentives for all managers to drive inter-property play. At the end of the transformation, Harrah's changed itself from a series of individually marketed properties to a national, customer-centric, data-driven powerhouse. By properly defining the vision for its brand and therefore for what type of company it would become, Harrah's was able to build brand architecture and invest its marketing dollars to full effect.

Brand architecture is the platform required to secure strategic market positions and drive sustained profitability for the firm. It includes the primary attributes of a brand—its image, the functional and emotional benefits delivered to customers. But as we saw with Neutrogena, the brand also includes the components that define how products must be formulated, manufactured, and distributed in order to deliver on the brand's promise. The positioning of the brand against competition and the target customers must be well defined. Like the architecture for a building, the schematic of the brand

155

describes each component and how it fits together to produce the end product—a brand asset that produces sustained profitability in the marketplace. The brand architecture also clearly defines the messages that customers take away from any interaction with that brand. Importantly, they must also describe these messages in ways that can be understood by the various functions of the enterprise. These functions deliver on the promise of the brand every day, with each activity reflecting directly or indirectly on the integrity of the brand. Communicating brand messaging across the firm was a key goal for Harrah's and is a vital part of developing successful brand architecture.

Fully Integrate Marketing into the Enterprise

In most organizations, the brand messages are not communicated effectively to the enterprise as a whole and marketing does not have the necessary level of influence over the vital brand-impacting activities of the rest of the organization. Too often there is insufficient feedback from other departments on how nonmarketing processes and policies impact the brand. The information flow between departments such as marketing, finance, HR, and operations is limited at best. Without more collaboration and a systematic way to control and measure brand impacts, companies can't possibly succeed in building and delivering great brands.

Integrate Marketing with Sales

American Express found that at any given time there were 300 to 500 marketing programs that their salespeople were expected to adopt and sell to prospects. Not surprisingly, the sales force complained of information overload. At the same time, products were becoming more complicated and sales cycles were lengthening. To solve this problem, American Express created a sales intelligence system that contained information on all the messaging and marketing programs that a salesperson needed. Then by submitting a simple request to the system, the salesperson received a printed agreement of all the marketing materials that they needed for the particular industry and business problem faced by their prospect.

American Express solved a problem that is all too common within business. Generally speaking, sales and marketing simply do not work well together. There are clashes in personality and each side believes the other does not deliver on its promise. Marketing believes salespeople are overly focused on quotas and not on learning and feeding back vital market information. Similarly, salespeople believe marketing is out of touch with the realities of carrying a bag and that marketing messages are not well tuned for their needs.

Marketing must focus on closer collaboration as well as the following objectives to better integrate with sales:

- Collaborate with sales to ensure messaging is sales ready.

- Ensure messages are easily accessed and information is digestible.

- Ensure information is deliverable in a format that is suitable for the way people sell and the type of prospect and solution being sold.

- Ensure marketing information is understandable by salespeople with different levels of training.

- Ensure marketing materials reflect the real problems of everyday customers.

- Ensure marketing materials reflect the conversations already going on between the sales force and customers.

Integrate Marketing with HR

Talent is the most vital asset of the modern firm, and strong brands attract talented people to the firm. By developing brand architecture and messaging that speaks to employees and potential employees, marketing can help in the vital task of securing the assets that will innovate, build, and sell the firm's products. By working more closely with HR, marketing can ensure marketing messages drive excitement in the employee base and create a magnet for outside talent.

Integrate Marketing with Operations

Decisions in manufacturing, inventory management, distribution, and even raw materials procurement directly impact the brand. For example, if the brand promises quality, saving money on raw materials can be highly detrimental. Similarly, chasing operational efficiencies can be harmful if the unique features of the product are compromised. In another example, if product availability and delivery reliability are attributes of the brand, lowering safety stock to reduce costs can be similarly harmful. As we saw with Neutrogena, great brands tend to be backed up with unique value chains. The activities in its value chain are different from other soap makers. In many ways they appear less efficient and more expensive. But viewed another way, they reflect investments in specific areas and help create unique attributes of the brand and long-term competitive advantage.

Integrate Marketing with Finance

A critical aspect of a more scientific approach to marketing is the ability to quantify marketing activities and measure results. This requires a close partnership with the finance department. As the ultimate corporate scorekeeper, finance holds the information marketing needs to assess past performance as a guide to current and future decisions. But finance will not necessarily track results in the way marketing needs them, and collaboration is required to ensure the departments are in synch. For example, marketing may require expenditures, revenues, and profit by campaign and by customer segment; but finance may track revenue, expenditure, and profit by product only. Often, gaining the more detailed perspective from finance involves analysis such as activity-based costing. Because such efforts are so time-consuming, they create barriers and make it unrealistic for marketers to access such data frequently. By collaborating on the key measures up-front, marketing can forge a partnership with finance and obtain the quantitative data it needs to run its activities with more accountability.

Measure and Optimize Marketing Investments

Marketing initiatives are investments that can provide tremendous returns for the business. Some of these investments will disappoint and some will return benefits far beyond expectations. But like a mutual fund manager, the key task for the marketer is to construct a portfolio of investments that has the best chance of achieving optimal returns. Many investments will be similar to ones made in the past or by others, and the history of results can guide expectations for current and future investments. Return on investment (ROI)-driven marketers know the expected value of investments they are about to make because they have access to historical results. This type of marketer creates a balanced portfolio with an expected outcome and then spends time tracking progress and results of the efforts.

The following tasks are key to ensure marketing investments are optimized:[5]

- Ensure investments support the firm's strategy and specific competitive advantages.

- Ensure investments support brand architectures.

- Create a portfolio of marketing investments.

- Develop expected outcomes based on historical results.

- Develop key metrics that indicate progress and results of investments.

- Develop nonfinancial metrics that serve as likely leading indicators of the progress of investments.

- Implement a consistent process for measuring progress and final results of investments.

- Implement a review process for assessing success of portfolio construction and expected value predictions.

As enterprise marketing management matures and takes its rightful place driving policy throughout the firm and defining customer experience, marketing and customer strategy will become highly integrated. They will become the keystone linking the firm's overall strategy with its policies and procedures for executing the strategy.

Key Points

- The departments of most firms do not coordinate well enough to produce seamless customer experience and interactions.

- This lack of coordination makes delivering tailored experiences for customers more difficult or impossible.

- As well as functional strategies for each department, companies should produce a customer strategy designed to marshal customer activity and differential treatments across the firm.

- More integrated and scientific marketing approaches are required and these are highly integrated with customer strategy.

Notes

1. Gareth Herschel, "PepsiAmericas Uncaps a Key to Customer Satisfaction." Stamford: Gartner, *www.gartner.com*, December 2, 2002.

2. Ranjay Gulati, "Bringing the Customer Back In: Going from Technology-Focused to Market-Focused Organizations." Evanston, IL: Kellogg Graduate School of Management, March 2002; and Dale L. Goodhue, Barbara H. Wixom, and Hugh J. Watson, "Managing customer relationships used to be easier," *MIS Quarterly*, June 2002.

3. Philip Kotler, Dipak C. Jain, and Suvit Maesincee, *Marketing Moves, 1st edition*. Cambridge: Harvard Business School Press, March 7, 2002.

4. Dave Sutton and Tom Klein, *Enterprise Marketing Management: The New Science of Marketing*. New York: John Wiley & Sons, May 2003.

5. Sutton and Klein, *Enterprise Marketing Management*.

Implementing CRM Successfully

In previous chapters, we showed how the lack of strategic alignment, customer insight, and coordination of customer priorities across functional areas leads to unsatisfactory returns on CRM investments. *Unfortunately, even when the right approaches are taken, companies can still fail due to faulty implementation.* As we saw in Chapter 2, there are many potential CRM pitfalls, including lack of executive attention, under-skilled teams, too little attention to business-process changes, implementations that are too large and unwieldy, over-emphasis on technology tasks, and failure to mitigate difficult organizational and political challenges.

The negative outcome of botched CRM implementations includes write-offs, earnings disappointments, budget and schedule overruns, and a pronounced lack of tangible business results. The material in this chapter describes how the rigorous approaches of leading companies should be combined with the implementation of Best Practices to ensure CRM is applied successfully within organizations. It shows how to get started, achieve alignment, and measure results.

Implementation Guidelines for Success

The following guidelines illustrate Best Practices needed to successfully implement a well-planned CRM initiative. These include:

- Attain executive sponsorship and alignment.

- Define the strategic context and business case.

- Build a balanced team.

- Align with customer strategy.

- Develop a roadmap.

- Implement rapidly.

- Address all aspects of change.

- Avoid technology traps.

Attain Executive Sponsorship and Alignment

The first step toward guaranteeing success for any strategic initiative is to generate enthusiastic support across the enterprise. Strategic Ideas often come from executive management, but just as often they originate at different levels within the firm. Obviously top-down ideas already have a sponsor but this does not necessarily mean they achieve alignment. Seasoned executives know that team alignment doesn't occur immediately. It is an ongoing process that requires consistent, honest, and accurate communication around a core set of key messages. Ideas generated at lower levels tend to lack both sponsorship and alignment and both are vital to success. Without senior executive backing, the initiative simply will not have sufficient voice in the senior ranks.

Most initiatives require tough choices and difficult changes that will significantly impact various parts of the business. Without senior support, a major change—like the launch of a CRM initiative—is extremely difficult to make.

Another obstacle to company-wide change management is the fact that large companies are typically organized by P&L business units. These units often have high degrees of autonomy and make their own decisions on pursuing strategic initiatives. Practically speaking, it is often unrealistic for senior management to dictate adoption of strategic changes at the business-unit level. Typically, the value of initiatives must be proved before P&L leaders will adopt them. As a result, the most pragmatic approach is for top management to gain up-front acceptance from a receptive subset of the P&L leaders. There are a number of ways to achieve broad-based agreement on major proposals. Several examples follow:

- At a British Petroleum division, leadership buy-in was obtained by presenting a study that described how the firm compared with rivals on key CRM capabilities. This report helped convince the executive team that CRM investments should be considered.

- At a leading mortgage banking firm, a study of internal customer data revealed new information about customer needs and profitability. The investigating team presented to management a number of hypotheses that recommended a more targeted approach to certain customers. The presentation resulted in management's agreement to test several of the hypotheses.

- A global consumer goods company faced commoditization of certain products. An enterprise-level senior executive felt pricing pressure could be defrayed by using CRM's customer-centric approaches as they would give the firm a better understanding of customer needs and help identify value-added products and services. The executive convened a workshop and invited representatives from the firm's businesses around the world. He also invited outside speakers and veterans of past CRM initiatives. This first step raised awareness of the need for customer-centric thinking, garnered a company-wide appreciation of challenges faced, and revealed thought leaders who were willing to pioneer ideas.

Both sponsorship and alignment require a concerted effort and neither will take hold overnight. Strategic initiatives that lack either or both characteristics will almost certainly fail. The following steps outline an effective approach for achieving successful alignment:

- Collect and analyze data about the current business situation.

- Compare current capabilities to competition.

- Conduct executive workshops to build idea awareness and generate hypotheses.

- Identify thought leaders among the business units who are willing to pioneer ideas.

- Generate communication plans, including core messages.

- Test hypotheses and use results to build momentum for the initiative.

In addition, an executive steering committee should be in place for the duration of the implementation. This group should consist of the top executive sponsors from the relevant areas of the business. Broad executive participation allows the implementation teams to review major issues like changes in risk/reward levels, plus it provides an opportunity to discuss and confirm strategic objectives on an ongoing basis.

Define the Strategic Context and Business Case

When approached properly, initial planning activities will produce well-defined goals for CRM initiatives. The scope and objectives of the program will state strategic advantages the firm wishes to strengthen, and the areas of Operational Effectiveness (OE) targeted for improvement. In addition, the plans will provide the implementation team with guidance on how to anchor the project. Planning will answer questions such as: Are the goals of the project transitional or transformational? Is the company making investments to strengthen strategy, or is the goal to automate existing processes, or to adopt a set of Best Practices? This information provides the critical background information teams need to ensure implementation decisions are aligned with the original goals of the initiative. We call this the *strategic context* for the initiative

Other useful context includes data justifying strategic or OE goals, assessments of strengths and weaknesses versus rivals, and information about trends in buying behavior or demand patterns. Other issues may include pertinent environmental factors, such as market trends or regulatory changes. The underlying data that informed the original planning decisions illustrates why initiatives are being undertaken in the first place. It serves as a reminder throughout the implementation process of what issues are being addressed and how to stay on track. Strategic context ensures that implementation decisions are not made in isolation or with incomplete information.

Most firms have done a poor job defining business cases and return on investment (ROI) models for their CRM initiatives. They implement CRM with lofty but unclear expectations that vary across the organization, with many areas assuming they will receive more benefit than is realistic. These missteps can be further aggravated by the propensity of most companies to bite off large-scale implementation efforts. The net result is that many classify their CRM implementations as disappointments. In most cases, it is difficult to measure the actual results because few companies actually benchmark their operations prior to launching initiatives.

By contrast, successful companies apply more rigor to defining and tracking business cases, by:

- Developing a robust cost/benefit model.

- Benchmarking current performance to create a point of comparison against which to measure improvements.

- Adopting a systematic approach for assessing the ROI impact of scope and implementation decisions.

- Generating measurement systems to track actual results.

Business case development is one of the CRM implementation's key activities because it forces examination of current and projected capabilities. While it is clearly a bad idea to invest without benchmarking the starting point and measuring results, many organizations still cut business case development from their project plans as they go down the CRM path. Most successful examples of business case development are based on smaller initiatives where results are easier to benchmark and track. Many companies insist on sticking with easily identifiable efficiency gains in producing the business case. However, for CRM to be leveraged strategically, the strategy-related benefits should also be identified. This type of modeling is more difficult but ultimately worthwhile. It can be achieved by using scenario techniques that project a range of possible outcomes.

Of course, results are measured once CRM is operational and this means having metrics and measurement systems in place. For example, Mexico-based bank Grupo Financiero Bital identified two key indicators for the success of its CRM initiative: total share of deposits and loans, together with share of new deposits and loans. Since 1999, share of deposits have grown from 9.6 to 12.7 percent and they are capturing 35 percent of new deposits. In addition, share of loans climbed from 7.2 to 14.6 percent and they captured 16 percent of new loans. Bital is the only Mexican bank to grow its share of the national market in this period.[1]

Build a Balanced Team

We have observed several common characteristics of successful CRM implementation teams:

- They are staffed with the firm's top performers.

- They have full cross-functional representation.

- They are not over-weighted with technology skills.

- Business process and change management experts are included on the team.

- The firm is disciplined about dedicating the needed time and internal resources.

- Executives and other business leaders are designated and assigned to the team.

As suggested, team leaders must be experienced employees with the ability to think critically and challenge the status quo, because ultimately this group will lead and implement changes throughout the organization. The team members should be high performers, creative, and sufficiently respected within the organization to help evangelize and enact change.

For a good example of how a team can help drive actual results from the outset, let's examine a project at Aventis, one of the world's leading providers of treatments for diabetes. The CRM program started with the establishment of a core team created by the CEO. He designed the team structure and mandated strong resource allocations to ensure team dedication and positive results. Team leaders included a project head and project leader, and the rest of the team included executives representing each of the company's global regions. Team members were required to dedicate 30 percent of their time to the team, attend team meetings, and create and implement each initiative. The program recognized that by using program creators as program implementers, buy-in for initiatives were automatically built into the system. As the firm's head of portfolio and sales management put it: "Down the road we will not have to win buy-in because we created it. You will not have to buy what you create."[2]

Align with Customer Strategy

In Chapter 6, we saw how companies defined their enterprise-wide plans for managing customers—alternatively called *customer strategy*—

in order to deliver consistent customer experiences across the enterprise. This definition provides the framework for how every customer is to be treated by each department.

If a customer strategy is not in place it should be established during planning and before significant CRM implementation efforts are undertaken. If already in place, the impact of some initiatives, such as targeting a new market or launching a new channel, might require a revision of the customer strategy. For example, this might result in the addition of order handling and delivery policies for online orders— both of which would also affect workloads and priorities within order entry, fulfillment, and finance. It might also require changes to customer support staff assignments, escalation procedures, and return policies associated with the new product launch. Many CRM initiatives involve changes in numerous policies and procedures across multiple departments. The customer strategy defines these impact points throughout the firm and is the starting point for assessing the impact of these initiatives.

Develop a Roadmap

For far-reaching initiatives, organizations need a visionary roadmap that describes the implementation stages over time. Painting a picture of the future provides a long-term perspective and ensures that everyone is on the same page and working toward a common goal. The roadmap also makes certain that initiatives are implemented in a measured and incremental way and allows the flexibility needed to adjust plans and limit exposure to risk.

The CRM roadmap describes a multistage schedule that promotes and facilitates the deployment of the new capabilities (combinations of people, process, and technology that deliver measurable value) in a logical and paced manner. In fulfilling its primary objective, the roadmap creates a definitive position for the organization that helps every individual and team member to work in unison, and ensures that each of these stakeholders expects similar outcomes from the project.

The strategy roadmap also defines how the organization builds and deploys new capabilities—such as a customer-centric sales and service model that generates quick financial returns. It illustrates the company's "release philosophy" on when to launch new capabilities and when to address change management. The strategy roadmap also describes internal and external factors such as the current economy, competitive threats, and internal resistance.

To support change management planning, the roadmap should also identify the internal company groups that will benefit from, or be impacted by, the strategy. It must also specify the sequence and program schedule for building and deploying the customer-centric capabilities based on realistic parameters. These should include priority and feasibility considerations such as industry cycles, market factors, budget considerations, operational or financial calendars, competing or complementary initiatives, technical constraints, and user-group readiness.

Notwithstanding the value of visionary roadmaps, the most important part of instituting these new ideas is to start from customer insight, begin with small initiatives, and let the success build momentum. Momentum is a powerful ally and the perception of progress will help identify and solve change management challenges.

Implement Rapidly

To reinforce a point made earlier, it is essential that firms take an incremental approach to initiatives, since the large-scale implementations of the past generally have been unsuccessful. For example, in order to target increases in sales volume, a firm might identify changes needed in territory alignment, pricing policies, and sales force automation technology. In the past, many firms attempted to rush the implementation of these changes in an effort to achieve gains across the entire sales force.

Alternatively, a "rapid-fire implementation" program could focus on making the changes within a single region. A firm might identify a 100-day initiative to implement the changes with a goal of increasing sales by 3 percent. Rapid-fire initiatives avoid costly failures, identify implementation pitfalls, and create a SWAT team atmosphere of quick change and close monitoring of results. In addition, the intense focus and short time frame have a number of other important benefits as they:

- Force people to set aside organizational politics.

- Hold everyone's attention and allow the initiative to sustain momentum.

- Mandate a tight rein on scope.

- Sharpen decision making.[3]

The consumer goods company referenced earlier recently created a series of rapid-fire, 100-day initiatives utilizing small, cross-functional teams. Programs included targeting more sales to a particular customer by collaborating closely with key suppliers, securing orders for a new product, and testing new distribution approaches. The firm's initial efforts were widely viewed as successful, generating around $8 million of revenue. The company has since expanded the program to include hundreds of employees, and is forecasting $50 million in revenue gains by year-end.[4]

By contrast, the cost of big-bang implementations gone awry can be staggering, as we saw in Chapter 2 with the Hershey and CIGNA Healthcare examples. To avoid these types of traps, organizations should define initiatives that can be quickly rolled out and measured. Broadly speaking, this is much the same process as that for leveraging customer insights as described in Chapter 4:

- Examine data.

- Generate hypotheses.

- Run rapid-fire pilot projects (experiments).

- Collect data on results.

- Make permanent improvements or modify idea.

Address All Aspects of Change: Organizational, Process, and Technology

Most organizations make the mistake of over-emphasizing the technology aspects of implementation when, in fact, the organizational, policy, and process changes almost always prove more challenging. CRM changes many of the firm's daily work activities and how people within the firm interact. New tools are implemented or old tools are used in different ways. New roles and skill sets are required, and existing roles and skill sets will be redefined. Significant change will impact thousands of people, making smooth adoption difficult within most organizations. Widespread resistance to change is common and an unenthusiastic reception can doom a CRM initiative.

Veterans of other initiatives such as ERP will recognize the importance of this section. However, CRM requires even more change management. With ERP implementations, employees are captive; meaning they often have little choice but to use the processes and tools to get their jobs done. When it comes to posting financial transactions or entering inventory or factory orders, there are few options for getting around it. This is often not the case with CRM where marketers, for example, can design and run a campaign based on gut feel, bypassing available data-analysis tools. In addition, sales people may only need to use a sales force automation (SFA) tool if a pipeline report is due. Typically, only call center staff handling service requests are captive, which in part explains the relative success organizations have had in implementing call centers versus other elements of CRM.

In the successful consumer-goods company projects mentioned earlier, the firm took pains to staff each initiative with the right mix of skills to ensure that organizational, policy, process, and technology changes could be affected across the various areas of the firm. They understood that successful execution requires many types of change and widespread buy-in.

In general, organizational change and process tasks dominate transformational initiatives, since programs with strategic goals involve implementing new activities or performing traditional activities in different ways. This means new roles, skills, or organizational structure may be required. The business processes associated with the new ideas often must be created. As a result, these types of initiatives contain proportionally more organizational and process effort than any other.

However, initiatives that are less focused on strategic objectives and more on adopting Best Practices tend to require significant process effort. When the firm is adopting Best Practices—such as those embedded in purchased software—the processes often differ significantly from current ones. Significant process definition and staff retraining is often required.

The executive sponsors of the CRM initiatives are the key to the organizational challenges. Without their wisdom, experience, influence, and rapt attention, these challenges will tend to overwhelm most initiatives. As the CRM implementation proceeds, these are the challenges that should occupy the forefront of the minds of project sponsors.

Avoid Technology Traps

It is important to re-emphasize that technology should play a supporting but not leading role in CRM initiatives. Only after the organizational, process, and policy changes have been identified should the enabling technologies be considered. Companies tend to overemphasize the importance of the technology components of their CRM initiatives and imagine the software is the key to achieving business results, when results come mainly from changes in the ways the business is run. Successful companies treat technology as what it is—a highly valuable enabler to be used in conjunction with fundamental business changes.

To avoid "technology traps" that many fall into, companies should adopt the following practices:

- Make key strategic, policy, and process decisions before committing to technology decisions.

- Don't rush into making enterprise-wide package decisions in order to lock in a "good per-seat deal" on the software. This tends to defocus the team, delays important strategic decisions, and leaves business unit leaders with the feeling that software is being forced upon them.

- Avoid letting technologists dominate decision making. Ensure decisions are balanced across all aspects of the initiative.

- Account for long-term maintenance of the CRM technology infrastructure. Software maintenance agreements can be costly. In addition, expensive and time-consuming upgrades and refinements are often needed.

- Take care not to overengineer technical designs. This dampens usability and system performance, and detracts time from the necessary change management efforts.

- Ensure that the quantity and level of packaged software functionality is not overerestimated. Many projects have failed due to overly optimistic assumptions of how "fully baked" a software package was.

- Never underestimate the complexity of integration among systems from different vendors. Many high-profile CRM failures tend to feature heavy integration between back-office and CRM systems. In project plans, emphasize design and testing of integration points.

- Prevent the over-configuration of software applications. Projects with bloated scope are not absorbed well by the organization, and tend to result in severe usability and performance problems.

- Spend enough time on usability and performance design and testing. These are the most visible and loathed of system shortcomings from a user's perspective.

- Allocate enough time for training and otherwise preparing end users and managers for the full impact of using new or modified tools.

Used properly, technology is a powerful tool that creates competitive advantage as well as operational effectiveness. But only a balanced program that integrates organization, process, policy, and technology efforts can achieve these goals.

In this chapter we have described a new approach to implementation: Well-balanced teams pursue rapid-fire initiatives to test new ideas, and the results are systematically measured, refined, and adopted. This more rigorous approach results in better accountability. Leaders would do well to heed the important lessons of the past. The follies of wasted investments and the wisdom of those leading companies that chose the right path are evident. Whether planning or implementing CRM initiatives, strategic focus, insight, rigor, and results orientation are the keys to enduring success.

Key Points

- With CRM initiatives, most companies bite off more scope than they can chew and fail to implement the initiatives successfully.

- Initial and ongoing executive and team alignment is the critical step in successfully implementing initiatives.

- Initiatives should be small in scope, tested first, and then adopted if demonstrably successful.

- Technology is generally overemphasized. It is an important enabler of CRM, but achieving success requires a balance of organizational policy and process as well as technology change.

Notes

1. Claudio Marcus and Tom Berg, "CRM Excellence Case Study: Grupo Financiero Bital." Stamford: Gartner, *www.gartner.com*, available as of February 3, 2004.

2. Lisa Smith, "CRM Management: Creating a Cross-Functional Approach," #4218, Best Practices, LLC, December 4, 2001.

3. Nadim F. Matta and Ronald N. Ashkenas, "Why Good Projects Fail Anyway," *Harvard Business Review*, #R0309H. Boston: Harvard Business School Press, September 1, 2003.

4. Matta and Ashkenas, "Why Good Projects Fail Anyway."

EPILOGUE

The Future of CRM

The outlook for CRM will continue to improve as companies take a measured and balanced approach to planning and implementation. As we've explored in this book, the failed projects of the past have wasted money and caused serious operational issues. However, shrill calls for the death of CRM are premature and unconstructive, given the pressing challenges organizations face in meeting increasing customer and competitive demands. Successful companies must continue to deliver consistent customer experiences, collect and analyze customer data, and leverage technologies that improve the speed and efficiency of sales, service, and marketing. CRM is a powerful tool that can help firms meet these challenges, but it can wreak havoc in untrained hands.

CRM is here to stay because organizations will strive for new and innovative ways to sell to and serve customers. New markets and ideas, upstart rivals, and emerging technologies will continue to provide a driving force for change. Unfortunately, the CRM we know today is mired in its sophomore jinx—the once promising prospect didn't live up to expectations and many are wondering what will become of it. Some will recall the similar difficulties faced by enterprise resource planning (ERP) software during its first wave.

Eventually, organizations learned how to avoid ERP's perils and harness its benefits, and it is likely that CRM will evolve in a similar pattern.

As we've seen from the examples in this book, there are few quick fixes. Firms must start with a review of ongoing CRM efforts to ensure they are helping to strengthen strategy. It is also key to take the first steps in organizing and mining data assets. The data contain nuggets of gold that are likely to reveal unconventional wisdom, illuminate profitable opportunities, and even shape the firm's future strategy. Approaching CRM strategically and leveraging company data are important first steps in capturing CRM's promise. However, there are also emerging areas within CRM that offer additional and important benefits. We believe that the next 10 years will represent CRM's second major phase—much as the late 1990s proved to be the second wave of ERP.

As CRM moves into its next generation, let's look at some of the trends and new benefits it will deliver. These can be summarized into six key areas:

1. New marketing approaches

2. Understanding financial metrics related to customers

3. New management approaches based on predictive analysis

4. Continuous optimization of operations

5. Leveraging emerging and specialized technologies

6. Harnessing the benefits of outsourcing

New Marketing Approaches

Marketing has largely been ignored during past CRM efforts, as organizations have most often focused on automating call centers and sales forces. CRM will help automate marketing processes in the future, but traditional marketing departments have problems that go well beyond lack of automation. They must reengineer themselves and take a more quantitative approach to planning and managing marketing investments. Too often, campaigns and promotions are launched based only on exciting creative ideas or with a business-as-usual attitude. But a quantitative approach allows marketers to run the function as a portfolio of investments, each with an associated expected return based on historical data. A fact-based, quantitative approach provides powerful support to the creative muscle that helps drive revenue and brand equity.

In response to these needs, organizations will redefine marketing processes and marketing's interactions with sales and the rest of the enterprise. Tighter planning and execution integration between departments will ensure customer experiences are consistent across every customer touch-point. This will enable everyone in the firm to contribute to growing the brand. Existing software vendors are beefing up the marketing elements of their suites and new vendors are emerging. We expect revamped marketing approaches to be a common, even leading, goal of CRM efforts over the coming years.

Understanding Financial Metrics Related to Customers

In most organizations there is too little understanding of the true profit contribution of various customer segments. In fact, when rigorous analysis is carried out, managers are often shocked to find that few customers are very profitable, and a large number are actually money-losing relationships. It doesn't have to be that way. By properly understanding the revenue and cost picture, firms can adjust how they interact with unprofitable customers and even turn many into solid contributors to the bottom line. Similarly, efforts can focus on turning high-potential segments into high achievers. The first step in rationalizing the profitability of the customer base is to identify the segments and track the key metrics associated with them.

Many CRM initiatives now start with customer segmentation and the analysis of customer profitability. In the future, firms will track the financial details of their customer operations more closely, allowing a full picture of where the company is wasting resources or underachieving. Customer-centric organizational models will better facilitate such tracking, and business applications, such as CRM and ERP, will be tailored to allow the capture and analysis of customer financial metrics.

New Management Approaches Based on Predictive Analysis

High performance companies almost seem able to see into the future. They accurately predict demand patterns, spot changes in customer needs, and detect trends in the marketplace. By capturing data early and predicting fluctuations, top firms respond fast to changing circumstances and emerging opportunities and, as a result, they perform better than their peers. In the future, firms will adopt the approaches of these successful companies. They will invest in infrastructure that better enables the collection and analysis of data, and create models that predict the future based on current and historical data. The centerpiece of these models will be more accurate demand forecasting. However, they will also include models such as those for predicting future profitability of certain markets, products, or customer segments, or the optimization of pricing and revenue management. Predictive management improves the quality of decisions throughout the business and helps firms to be highly responsive to changes. All firm activities will be designed to quickly react to changing demand environments. For example, accurate predictions will drive capacity decisions throughout the business, including staff, warehouse space, transportation capacity, and inventory. Additionally, real-time updates on ordering trends resulting from marketing campaigns will allow for automated adjustments of production capacity and supply chain ordering.

Instead of the traditional sequential plan-execution cycle, companies will emulate leaders by continuously monitoring for changes, generating predictions, and refining execution plans.

Traditionally, CRM has provided a means to capture customer information but not the ability to analyze it or create predictive models. As we know, many firms have implemented CRM without a plan for tapping the vastly enriched sources of customer data that's at their fingertips. For the most part, firms now have the transaction layer that facilitates data capture, but in the future they must build an analytics layer to leverage this data. This build-out of analytics capability will be a major secular trend within information technology and information management. CRM applications are beginning to provide some analytical functionality around forecasting, sales, marketing, and service areas, together with the tools to tightly link CRM with supply chain and demand planning systems and processes. In the future, capabilities to capture data and analyze across company borders will emerge, vastly increasing the accuracy of predictive models.

Continuous Optimization of Operations

As discussed earlier in this book, CRM should strengthen an organization's competitive advantages. Although information technology has certainly delivered tremendous efficiencies in the past, it remains underutilized as a tool for reinforcing strategic positioning. The next wave of CRM will see organizations applying CRM principles and tools in rifle shot rather than shotgun fashion. CRM will be used to optimize business processes and activities in ways that not only increase efficiencies but also strengthen competitive advantages. The approaches are specific to each firm but often include bolstering traditional strengths such as unique product development, strong customer service and relationships, proprietary information or technologies, and the conduct of distinctive physical activities. Optimization is a continuous process that provides steady results but is never really completed. In fact, in addition to CRM tools, it is likely that most information technology projects will be implemented in this strategic way going forward.

A key component of optimizing operations is to first capture detailed performance information. Data analysis tools will look to address areas such as inefficient capital usage, production order hold up, product return patterns, or customer service bottlenecks. These tools may also help spot opportunities to optimize sales to certain types of customers. The optimized value chain is highly internally integrated, tightly linked to key suppliers and customers, utilizes real-time information, and features particular uniqueness around the key activities that provide competitive advantage for the firm.

Leveraging Emerging and Specialized Technologies

Emerging technologies will provide innovative ways to reach and add value for customers, integrate operations, interpret data, and predict the future. For example, wireless technologies give customers in many industries another channel option for buying and customer service. This is especially important in verticals such as financial services and logistics, where real-time status can provide significant customer value. Mobile devices and communications technologies have already been added to CRM applications to address these emerging needs.

Similarly, the Internet will continue its growth in commercial and societal importance. For some demographic groups, the Internet is now the dominant channel for news and communications, and emerging technologies promise to increase its power and reach. XML (extensible markup language) has become the universal standard for representing data, and web services technologies will provide standards for flexibly integrating applications within and across company borders. On the backs of these technologies and related innovations, a new, more intelligent Internet will emerge. This Internet will greatly enhance the ability of software applications to intelligently decipher web content, leading to much more effective web-searching and richer consumer and business-to-business interactions. More precise searches, better anticipation of user needs, and greater automation of interactions through mini-applications known as web-bots will become common. Customers are already keenly using the Internet to access their accounts, make inquiries, and pay bills. The promise of richer, faster interactions will drive increased demand for deeper Internet offerings.

In addition, instant messaging will significantly impact customer communications. Within many organizations today, instant messaging is a highly popular communications tool amongst the staff. Faster, spam-free, and slicker than email, it allows teams to collaborate in real time using quick, easy-to-manage conversation streams. By applying instant messaging, a company's customer interactions around product configuration, resolution of service issues, joint decision making, and collaboration on product design, all become cheaper, quicker, and more practical.

Another emerging technology, Radio Frequency Identification (RFID), promises to dramatically improve tracking of inventory and other assets, by imbedding inexpensive microchips into raw materials, products, and equipment. CRM tools will harness RFID, allowing quick and cheap tracking of inventory within distribution channels, and remote monitoring of product and machinery status at customer locations.

In addition to these emerging technologies, packaged business applications (such as the major CRM platforms) are likely to evolve significantly over the coming years. Two main trends are the emergence of industry-specific package variations and greater integration and automation of processes across the enterprise. Vertical varieties will increase the availability and depth of industry-specific tools. In the past, to get industry-specific functionality, the package had to be customized during implementation by people who understood both the technical and industry aspects. This was often an expensive task that increased the risk of defects and performance problems. In the future, built-in industry-specific functionality will significantly increase the speed and decrease the cost of implementation.

However, this prediction comes with a cautionary note. The availability of specific standard functionality increases the temptation for organizations to adopt the standard Best Practices being represented by the software. As noted during the discussion on anchoring in Chapter 2, this can be a good thing in some cases. But it many cases it blurs the distinctive elements of the firm's operations. Care must be taken to retain (and strengthen) competitive advantages while harnessing best practices where it makes sense.

In the past, CRM applications have been focused purely on automating front-office tasks, which created the need for significant integration with back-office systems such as ERP. Unfortunately, complex integration introduced failure points and performance issues and was a major contributor to implementation failures. The realization that many processes and departments impact customer interactions has led vendors to take a broader perspective about how their applications are architected. Instead of selling a collection of standard but customizable front-office applications, they are providing a web-services-based architecture that allows front-office, back-office, and external software components to be customized and integrated in a tightly knit fashion. Using this approach, multiple software systems can more easily interact in real time—within and across corporate boundaries. It also allows companies to monitor processes that span departments and firm borders, ensuring far better control and tracking of customer interactions. This integrated, componentized approach fits well with our focused-implementation recommendations and allows organizations to purchase software components from multiple vendors without incurring excessive maintenance costs.

Harnessing the Benefits of Outsourcing

Financial benefits coupled with technology innovations, such as browsers, software integration standards, and faster access speeds, have accelerated the outsourcing trend in many industries. Entire functions of the firm, including payroll, benefits administration, and customer service call centers can now be managed and operated by third-party vendors. This frees up resources and management attention to focus on other more "mission-critical" areas. Outsourcing CRM-related functions such as marketing or customer service is possible but problematic, as lowered costs achieved through outsourcing these areas may be offset by loss of control over critical customer interactions and opportunities to capture data.

Outsourcing firms typically provide service based on best practices for a given function, so for them, the economics work best when they can provide similar services to multiple clients. Outsourcing can result in compelling cost savings for certain areas of a business, but is not a good idea for activities that are key to the firm's competitive advantage. Since many customer-related activities are critical to competitive advantage, outsourcing, as attractive as it may be from a financial perspective, must be approached very cautiously.

However, some interesting outsourcing opportunities are emerging within the CRM space. These include utilizing outside vendors to manage and operate CRM software applications on behalf of the organization. In these situations, users simply log onto the applications over the Internet and use them as needed. The vendor maintains the company's data with all the necessary security. This approach is particularly suitable when limited customization is required. Some vendors have introduced a pay-per-use scheme where firms have access to IT infrastructure and applications and pay by volume of use.

Another emerging CRM outsourcing opportunity is the concept of managed analytics. In this case, a highly-specialized outside vendor provides sophisticated data analysis services. These vendors analyze a firm's data—such as historical customer purchase records—then report back patterns, predictions, and recommendations. These services provide an excellent way for firms to leverage their data assets and generate unique insight.

In conclusion, these are some of the ways in which CRM will evolve in the future, and it is clear that the next generation will bring further opportunities to add value for customers, strengthen competitive advantage, and improve efficiencies. However, the past presents a clear picture of the risks and costs associated with faulty approaches. CRM's powerful ideas and tools must be carefully harnessed, but by approaching it strategically and implementing it in focused ways, CRM is sure to drive long-term business gains.

Index